Advance Praise for
Burn It Down

"The twenty-two essays collected in *Burn It Down* are **a gift of sanity and clear-eyed moral vision** in an increasingly degraded moral world. This book galvanizes women's collective and individual rage, even as it redefines how we could and should understand that anger—and ourselves."
> —Lacy M. Johnson, author of
> *The Reckonings* and *The Other Side*

"*Burn It Down* is deeply affirming for any woman who has struggled with anger in this difficult world. **There is no judgment here; only alchemy.**"
> —Kelly Sundberg, author of *Goodbye, Sweet Girl*

"*Burn It Down* is a potent literary offering—a revolution born within the collective rage—expressed, unleashed, sublimated, and capsuled to honor our feminist legacy. Scorched earth speaks through these brilliant women who teach us that vulnerability and ire writ large will save those who have been shamed and condemned. **Glorious, punk as hell, and utterly necessary.**"
> —Sophia Shalmiyev,
> award-winning author of *Mother Winter*

"Powerful and provocative, this collection is an instructive read for anyone seeking to understand the many faces—and pains—of **womanhood in 21st-century America.**"
> —*Kirkus Reviews*

Burn It Down

Burn It Down

WOMEN WRITING ABOUT ANGER

Edited by

LILLY DANCYGER

SEAL PRESS
New York

AURORA PUBLIC LIBRARY

Cover design by Kimberly Glyder
Cover image © iStock.com/Ales_Utovko

Seal Press
Hachette Book Group
1290 Avenue of the Americas, New York, NY 10104
www.sealpress.com
@sealpress

Printed in the United States of America

First Edition: October 2019

Published by Seal Press, an imprint of Perseus Books, LLC, a subsidiary of Hachette Book Group, Inc. The Seal Press name and logo is a trademark of the Hachette Book Group.

The Hachette Speakers Bureau provides a wide range of authors for speaking events. To find out more, go to www.hachettespeakersbureau.com or call (866) 376-6591.

The publisher is not responsible for websites (or their content) that are not owned by the publisher.

Print book interior design by Trish Wilkinson

Library of Congress Cataloging-in-Publication Data has been applied for.

ISBNs: 978-1-58005-893-3 (hardcover), 978-1-58005-894-0 (ebook)

LSC-C

10 9 8 7 6 5 4 3 2 1

Contents

Contents

Contents

Introduction

LILLY DANCYGER

Throughout history, angry women have been called harpies, bitches, witches, and whores. They've been labeled hysterical, crazy, dangerous, delusional, bitter, jealous, irrational, emotional, dramatic, vindictive, petty, hormonal; they've been shunned, ignored, drugged, locked up, and killed; kept in line with laws and threats and violence, and with insidious, far-reaching lies about the very nature of what it means to be a woman—that a woman should aspire to be a lady, and that ladies don't get angry.

Millennia of conditioning is hard to unlearn.

Even when asked specifically to write about their anger, many of the women in this book described it at first from a safe distance, explaining coolly and calmly what they were angry about. They were so accustomed to having to rationally justify any emotion they might feel, while making sure not to actually display that emotion, that even in a book about anger, a big part of the editing process was me saying, "It's okay, get angry," and pushing writers to put their anger on the page.

The more that happened, the more I realized that was what I really wanted this book to be, I wanted this to be a place where our anger could live, a place for us to take up space after generations of being told to shrink, to rage after a lifetime of being told to behave. I wanted these pages to sizzle and smoke with women's awesome rage, no longer tucked away or extinguished, but right here on the surface—so get ready or get out of the way.

That meant something a little different for each writer. Essays in this collection explore the borders where anger meets other emotions: Erin Khar on when anger turns into guilt, Megan Stielstra on when fear turns into anger, and Marissa Korbel on when anger masquerades as sadness through involuntary rage tears. Others delve into the ways that anger intersects with identity, and how some women's anger is seen as more socially acceptable than others': Shaheen Pasha on the complicated anger of being a Muslim woman in America, Keah Brown on surviving the anger she's felt at herself and her disability, Samantha Riedel on experiencing anger differently before and after gender transition, and Monet Patrice Thomas on the ways that Black women, especially, are not allowed to express anger. And many describe the ways that women, brilliant alchemists that they are, have found to turn their anger into whatever they need it to be—strength, motivation, protection, healing. Some of the essays in this collection rage like wildfire, some smolder like embers, some glow like heated, metal, but they all radiate the heat of women bringing their anger out of hiding and into the open air.

There has been so much discussion recently of the power of women's anger, how it can be harnessed as a political engine, how it's been repressed for too long and is now going to erupt like a volcano and change the landscape of society for the better. And I'm as swept up in the revolutionary catharsis of our communal outpouring as the next girl, as ready to take a stand, to say "no more," to say "fuck you," and to say "me too."

But amid all of this talk *about* women's anger, as an idea, a force, a tool, I wanted to also look at that anger on its own terms, to give writers an opportunity to express and explore their anger, not as a means to an end but for its own sake. Our anger doesn't have to be useful to deserve a voice. Just as women who are so often reduced to sexual objects or baby-makers, caregivers, mothers, virgins, and whores, deserve to be considered as whole individuals on their own terms and for their own sakes, I wanted to give their anger space to exist solely for itself, without being packaged and used for someone else's gain. That's what this anthology is for.

There is so much to be angry about. I'm angry that we're destroying the planet and dooming ourselves to an unlivable future; angry that profits are prioritized over human lives; angry that racism is such a huge and deadly part of nearly every aspect of society, but still so many refuse to see it; angry that violence against women constricts the edges of our lives until we're crouched down seeking safety that doesn't exist; and angry that willful ignorance and misinformation have taken over political discourse so that it feels impossible to convince so many people that any of this is a problem.

Every woman I know is angry.

But this anthology is not about the things that make us angry; it's about us, and all the many ways we feel and live with our anger. There have been times in my life when my anger has made me small and hard and brittle, and there have been times when it's made me expansive and unstoppable, like fire. There have been times when my anger was frantic, sharp like splinters, shattering out in every direction—like when I was a teenager grieving the loss of my father by raging at the world, getting drunk and high first thing in the morning, getting into fistfights on the street, stealing, vandalizing, dropping out of high school, and transforming myself into a scantily clad, malnourished middle finger flying in the face of anyone who crossed my path. But lately, my anger is deep and wide and steady, not as immediately visible under the surface of my put-together life, but just as present. Lately, my anger is a place inside myself that I breathe into to make myself larger, taking up space and making space for others, by refusing to let my boundaries be ignored, by standing up for women in trouble, by stoking the fires of the incredible writers in this collection and bringing their work, and their anger, into the world as a salve for all the other angry women out there.

This anthology is an invitation. It is twenty-two writers saying to you what I said to them: "It's okay, get angry." Come rage with us. Our collective silence-breaking will make us larger, expansive, like fire, ready to burn it all down.

Lungs Full of Burning

LESLIE JAMISON

For years, I described myself as someone who wasn't prone to anger. "I don't get angry," I said. "I get sad." I believed this inclination was mainly about my personality—that sadness was a more natural emotion for me than anger, that I was somehow built this way. It's easy to misunderstand the self as private, when it's rarely private at all: it's always a public artifact, never fixed, perpetually sculpted by social forces. In truth, I was proud to describe myself in terms of sadness rather than anger. Why? Sadness seemed more refined and more selfless—as if you were holding the pain inside yourself rather than making someone else deal with its blunt-force trauma.

But a few years ago, I started to get a knot in my gut at the canned cadences of my own refrain: I don't get angry. I get sad. At the shrillest moments of our own self-declarations—I am X, I am not Y—we often hear in that tinny register another truth, lurking expectantly, and begin to realize there are things about ourselves we don't yet know. By which I mean that at a certain point, I started to suspect I was angrier than I thought.

Of course it wasn't anger when I was four years old and took a pair of scissors to my parents' couch—wanting so badly to destroy something, whatever I could. Of course it wasn't anger when I was sixteen and my boyfriend broke up with me, and I cut up the inside of my own ankle—wanting so badly to destroy something, whatever I could. Of course it wasn't anger when I was thirty-four and fighting with my husband, when I screamed into a pillow after he left the house so our daughter wouldn't hear, then threw my cellphone across the room and spent the next ten minutes searching for it under the bed, and finally found it in a small pile of cat vomit. Of course it wasn't anger when, during a faculty meeting early in my teaching days, I distributed statistics about how many female students in our department had reported instances of sexual harassment the year before: more than half of them.

A faculty member grew indignant and insisted that most of those claims probably didn't have any basis. I clenched my fists. I struggled to speak. It wasn't that I could say for sure what had happened in each of those cases—of course I couldn't, they were just anonymous numbers on the page—but their sheer volume seemed horrifying. It demanded attention. I honestly hadn't expected that anyone would resist these numbers or force me to account for why it was important to look at them. The scrutiny of the room made me struggle for words just when I needed them most. It made me dig my nails into my palm. What was that emotion? It was not sadness. It was rage.

The phenomenon of female anger has often been turned against itself, the figure of the angry woman reframed as threat—not the one who has been harmed, but the one bent on harming. She conjures a lineage of threatening archetypes: the harpy and her talons, the witch and her spells, the medusa and her writhing locks. The notion that female anger is unnatural or destructive is learned young; children report perceiving displays of anger as more acceptable from boys than from girls. According to a review of studies of gender and anger written in 2000 by Ann M. Kring, a psychology professor at the University of California, Berkeley, men and women self-report "anger episodes" with comparable degrees of frequency, but women report experiencing more shame and embarrassment in their aftermath. People are more likely to use words like "bitchy" and "hostile" to describe female anger, while male anger is more likely to be described as "strong." Kring reported that men are more likely to express their anger by physically assaulting objects or verbally attacking other people, while women are more likely to cry when they get angry, as if their bodies are forcibly returning them to the appearance of the emotion—sadness— with which they are most commonly associated.

A 2016 study found that it took longer for people to correctly identify the gender of female faces displaying an angry expression, as if the emotion had wandered out of its natural habitat by finding its way to their features. A 1990 study conducted by the psychologists Ulf Dimberg and L. O. Lundquist found that when female faces are recognized as angry, their expressions are rated as more hostile than comparable expressions on the faces of men—as if their violation of social expectations had already made their anger seem more extreme, increasing its volume beyond what could be tolerated.

In *What Happened*, her account of the 2016 presidential election, Hillary Clinton describes the pressure not to come across as angry during the course of her entire political career—"a lot of people recoil from an angry woman," she writes—as well as her own desire not to be consumed by anger after she lost the race, "so that the rest of my life wouldn't be spent like Miss Havisham from Charles Dickens's *Great Expectations*, rattling around my house obsessing over what might have been." The specter of Dickens's ranting spinster—spurned and embittered in her crumbling wedding dress, plotting her elaborate revenge—casts a long shadow over every woman who dares to get mad.

If an angry woman makes people uneasy, then her more palatable counterpart, the sad woman, summons sympathy more readily. She often looks beautiful in her suffering: ennobled, transfigured, elegant. Angry women are messier. Their pain threatens to cause more collateral damage. It's as if the prospect of a woman's anger harming other people threatens to rob her of the social capital she has gained by being wronged. We are most comfortable with female anger when it promises to regulate itself, to refrain from recklessness, to stay civilized.

Consider the red-carpet clip of Uma Thurman that went viral in November 2017 during the initial swell of sexual harassment accusations. The clip doesn't actually show Thurman's getting angry. It shows her very conspicuously refusing to get angry. After commending the Hollywood women who had spoken out about their experiences of sexual assault, she said that she was "waiting to feel less angry" before she spoke herself. It was curious that Thurman's public declarations were lauded as a triumphant vision of female anger, because the clip offered precisely the version of female anger that we've long been socialized to produce and accept: not the spectacle of female anger unleashed, but the spectacle of female anger restrained, sharpened to a photogenic point. By withholding the specific story of whatever made her angry, Thurman made her anger itself the story—and the raw force of her struggle not to get angry on that red carpet summoned the force of her anger even more powerfully than its full explosion would have, just as the monster in a movie is most frightening when it only appears offscreen.

This was a question I considered quite frequently as the slew of news stories accrued that fall: How much female anger has been lurking offscreen? How much anger has been biding its time and biting its tongue, wary of being pathologized as hysteria or dismissed as paranoia? And what of my own vexed feelings about all this female anger? Why were they even vexed? It seemed a failure of moral sentiment or a betrayal of feminism, as if I were somehow siding with the patriarchy, or had internalized it so thoroughly I couldn't even spot the edges of its toxic residue. I intuitively embraced and supported other women's anger but struggled to claim my own. Some of this had to do with the ways I'd been lucky—I had experienced all kinds of gendered aggression, but nothing equivalent to the horror stories so many other women have lived through. But it also had to do with an abiding aversion to anger that still festered like rot inside me. In what I had always understood as self-awareness—I don't get angry. I get sad—I came to see my complicity in the logic that has trained women to bury their anger or perform its absence.

For a long time, I was drawn to "sad lady" icons: the scribes and bards of loneliness and melancholy. As a certain kind of slightly morbid, slightly depressive, slightly self-intoxicated, deeply predictable, preemptively apologetic literary fan-girl, I loved Sylvia Plath. I was obsessed with her obsession with her own blood ("What a thrill . . . that red plush") and drawn to her suffering silhouette: a woman abandoned by her cheating husband and ensnared by the gendered double standards of domesticity. I attached myself to the mantra of her autobiographical avatar Esther Greenwood, who lies in a bathtub in *The Bell Jar*, bleeding during a rehearsal of a suicide attempt, and later stands at a funeral listening "to the old brag of my heart. I am, I am, I am." Her attachment to pain—her own and others'—was also a declaration of identity. I wanted to get it tattooed on my arm.

Whenever I listened to my favorite female singers, it was easier for me to sing along to their sad lyrics than their angry ones. It was easier to play Ani DiFranco on repeat, crooning about heartbreak—"Did I ever tell you how I stopped eating / when you stopped calling me?"—than it was to hear her fury and her irritation at the ones who stayed sad and quiet in her shadow: "Some chick says / Thank you for saying all the things I never do / I say, you know / The thanks I get is to take all the shit for you."

I kept returning to the early novels of Jean Rhys, whose wounded heroines flopped around dingy rented rooms in various European capitals, seeking solace from their heartbreak, staining cheap comforters with their wine. Sasha, the heroine of *Good Morning, Midnight*—the most famous of these early picaresques of pain—resolves to drink herself to death and manages, mainly, to cry her way across Paris. She cries at cafés, at bars, in her lousy hotel room. She cries at work. She cries in a fitting room. She cries on the street. She cries near the Seine. The closing scene of the novel is a scene of terrifying passivity: she lets a wraithlike man into her bed because she can't summon the energy to stop him, as if she has finally lost touch with her willpower entirely. In life, Rhys was infamous for her sadness, what one friend called "her gramophone-needle-stuck-in-a-groove thing of going over and over miseries of one sort and another." Even her biographer called her one of the greatest self-pity artists in the history of English fiction.

It took me years to understand how deeply I had misunderstood these women. I'd missed the rage that fueled Plath's poetry like a ferocious gasoline, lifting her speakers (sometimes literally) into flight: "Now she is flying / More terrible than she ever was, red / Scar in the sky, red comet / Over the engine that killed her—the mausoleum, the wax house." The speaker becomes a scar—this irrefutable evidence of her own pain—but this scar, in turn, becomes a comet: terrible and determined, soaring triumphant over the instruments of her own supposed destruction. I'd always been preoccupied with the pained disintegration of Plath's speakers, but once I started looking, I saw the comet trails of their angry resurrections everywhere, delivering their unapologetic fantasies of retribution: "Out of the ash / I rise with my red hair / And I eat men like air."

I'd loved Rhys for nearly a decade before I read her final novel, *Wide Sargasso Sea*, a reimagining of Charlotte Brontë's *Jane Eyre* whose whole plot leads inexorably toward an act of destructive anger: the mad first wife of Mr. Rochester burns down the English country manor where she has been imprisoned in the attic for years. In this late masterpiece, the heroines of Rhys's early novels—heartbroken, drunk, caught in complicated choreographies of passivity—are replaced by an angry woman with a torch, ready to use the master's tools to destroy his house.

It wasn't that these authors were writing exclusively about female anger rather than female sorrow; their writing holds both states of feeling. *Wide Sargasso Sea* excavates the deep veins of sadness running beneath an otherwise opaque act of angry destruction, and Plath's poems are invested in articulating the complicated affective braids of bitterness, irony, anger, pride, and sorrow that others often misread as monolithic sadness. "They explain people like that by saying that their minds are in watertight compartments, but it never seemed so to me," Rhys herself once wrote. "It's all washing about, like the bilge in the hold of a ship."

It has always been easier to shunt female sadness and female anger into the "watertight compartments" of opposing archetypes rather than acknowledge the ways they run together in the cargo hold of every female psyche. Near the end of the biopic *I, Tonya,* Tonya Harding's character explains: "America, they want someone to love, but they want someone to hate." The timing of the film's release, in late 2017, seemed cosmically apt. It resurrected a definitional prototype of female anger—at least for many women like me, who came of age during the 1990s—at the precise moment that so many women were starting to get publicly, explicitly, unapologetically angry.

Harding was an object of fascination not just because of the soap opera she dangled before the public gaze—supposedly conspiring with her ex-husband and an associate to plan an attack on her rival figure skater Nancy Kerrigan—but also because she and Kerrigan provided a yin and yang of primal female archetypes. As a vision of anger—uncouth and unrestrained, the woman everyone loved to hate, exploding at the judges when they didn't give her the scores she felt she deserved—Harding was the perfect foil for the elegant suffering of Kerrigan, sobbing in her lacy white leotard. Together they were a duo impossible to turn away from: the sad girl and the mad girl. Wounded and wicked. Their binary segregated one vision of femininity we adored (rule-abiding, delicate, hurting) from another we despised (trashy, whiny, angry). Harding was strong; she was poor; she was pissed off; and eventually, in the narrative embraced by the public, she turned those feelings into violence. But I, Tonya illuminates what so little press coverage at the time paid attention to: the perfect storm of violence that produced Harding's anger in the first place—her mother's abuse and her husband's. Which is to say: no woman's anger is an island.

When the Harding and Kerrigan controversy swept the media, I was ten years old. Their story was imprinted onto me as a series of reductive but indelible brushstrokes: one woman shouting at the media, another woman weeping just beyond the ice rink. But after watching I, Tonya and realizing how much these two women had existed to me as ideas, rather than as women, I did what any reasonable person would do: I Googled "Tonya and Nancy" obsessively. I Googled: "Did Tonya ever apologize to Nancy?" I Googled: "Tonya Harding boxing career?" and discovered that it effectively began with her 2002 "Celebrity Boxing" match against Paula Jones—two women paid to perform the absurd caricatures of vengeful femininity the public had projected onto them, the woman who cried harassment versus the woman who bashed kneecaps.

In the documentaries I watched, I found Harding difficult to like. She comes off as a self-deluded liar with a robust victim complex, focused on her own misfortune to the exclusion of anyone else's. But what does the fact that I found Harding "difficult to like" say about the kind of women I'm comfortable liking? Did I want the plotline to be that the woman who has survived her own hard life—abusive mother, abusive husband, enduring poverty—also emerges with a "likable" personality: a plucky spirit, a determined work ethic, and a graceful, self-effacing relationship to her own suffering?

The vision of Harding in *I, Tonya* is something close to the opposite of self-effacing. The film even includes a fantastical reenactment of the crime, which became popularly known as the "whack heard round the world," in which Harding stands over Kerrigan's cowering body, baton raised high above her head, striking her bloody knee until Harding turns back toward the camera—her face defiant and splattered with Kerrigan's blood. Even though the attack was actually carried out by a hired hit man, this imagined scene distills the version of the story that America became obsessed with, in which one woman's anger leaves another woman traumatized.

But America's obsession with these two women wasn't that simple. Another story rose up in opposition. In this shadow story, Harding wasn't a monster but a victim, an underdog unfairly vilified, and Kerrigan was a crybaby who made too much of her pain. In a 2014 Deadspin essay, "Confessions of a Tonya Harding Apologist," Lucy Madison wrote: "She represented the fulfillment of an adolescent revenge fantasy—my adolescent revenge fantasy, the one where the girl who doesn't quite fit in manages to soar over everyone's bullshit without giving up a fraction of her prerogative—and I could not have loved her more." When Kerrigan crouched sobbing on the floor near the training rink, right after the attack (*Newsweek* described it as "the sound of one dream breaking"), she famously cried out: "Why? Why? Why?" But when *Newsweek* ran the story on its cover, it printed the quote as: "Why Me?" The single added word turned her shock into keening self-pity.

These two seemingly contradictory versions of Harding and Kerrigan—raging bitch and innocent victim, or bad-girl hero and whiny crybaby—offered the same cutout dolls dressed in different costumes. The entitled weeper was the unacceptable version of a stoic victim; the scrappy underdog was the acceptable version of a raging bitch. At first glance, they seemed like opposite stories, betraying our conflicted collective relationship to female anger—that it's either heroic or uncontrollably destructive—and our love-hate relationship with victimhood itself: we love a victim to hurt for but grow irritated by one who hurts too much. Both stories, however, insisted upon the same segregation: A woman couldn't hurt and be hurt at once.

She could be either angry or sad. It was easier to outsource those emotions to the bodies of separate women than it was to acknowledge that they reside together in the body of every woman.

Ten years ago in Nicaragua, a man punched me in the face on a dark street. As I sat on a curb afterward—covered in my own blood, holding a cold bottle of beer against my broken nose—a cop asked me for a physical description of the man who had just mugged me. Maybe twenty minutes later, a police vehicle pulled up: a pickup truck outfitted with a barred cage in the back. There was a man in the cage.

"Is this him?" the cop asked. I shook my head, horrified, acutely aware of my own power—realizing, in that moment, that simply saying I was hurt could take away a stranger's liberty. I was a white woman, a foreigner volunteering at a local school, and I felt ashamed of my own familiar silhouette: a vulnerable white woman crying danger at anonymous men lurking in the shadows. I felt scared and embarrassed to be scared. I felt embarrassed that everyone was making such a fuss. One thing I did not feel was anger.

That night, my sense of guilt—my shame at being someone deemed worthy of protection, and at the ways that protection might endanger others—effectively blocked my awareness of my own anger. It was as if my privilege outweighed my vulnerability, and that meant I wasn't entitled to any anger at all. But if I struggled to feel entitled to anger that night in Nicaragua, I have since come to realize that the real entitlement has never been anger; it has always been its absence. The aversion to anger I had understood in terms of temperament or intention was, in all honesty, also a luxury. When the Black feminist writer and activist Audre Lorde described her anger as a life-long response to systemic racism, she insisted upon it as a product of the larger social landscape rather than private emotional ecology: "I have lived with that anger, on that anger, beneath that anger, on top of that anger . . . for most of my life."

After the Uma Thurman clip went viral, the Trinidadian journalist Stacy-Marie Ishmael tweeted: "*interesting* which kinds of women are praised for public anger. I've spent my whole career reassuring people this is just my face." Michelle Obama was dogged by the label of "angry Black woman" for the duration of her husband's time in office. Scientific research has suggested that the experience of racism leads African Americans to suffer from higher blood pressure than white Americans and has hypothesized that this disparity arises from the fact that they accordingly experience more anger and are simultaneously expected to suppress it. During the 2018 US Open final, the tennis superstar Serena Williams was chided and fined for expressions of anger that wouldn't necessarily get other players in trouble (she called the umpire a "thief"); but as law professor Trina Jones put it, responding to the incident: "Black women are not supposed to push back and when they do, they're deemed to be domineering. Aggressive.

Threatening." For Williams, this is part of a larger pattern: in 2009, Williams was fined over $80,000 for an angry outburst against a lineswoman; and in 2011, Gretchen Carlson, a Fox anchor at the time, called another one of Williams's angry outbursts a symbol of "what's wrong with our society today." Carlson, of course, has since come to embody a certain brand of female empowerment: one of the leading voices accusing the late Fox News chairman Roger Ailes of sexual harassment, she recently published a book called *Be Fierce: Stop Harassment and Take Your Power Back.* But the portrait on its cover—of a fair-skinned, blond-haired woman smiling slightly in a dark turtleneck—reminds us that fierceness has always been more palatable from some women than from others.

What good is anger, anyway? The philosopher Martha Nussbaum invokes Aristotle's definition of anger as "a response to a significant damage" that "contains within itself a hope for payback" to argue that anger is not only "a stupid way to run one's life" but also a corrosive public force, predicated on the false belief that payback can redress the wrongdoing that inspired it. She points out that women have often embraced the right to their own anger as a "vindication of equality," part of a larger project of empowerment, but that its promise as a barometer of equality shouldn't obscure our vision of its dangers. In this current moment of ascendant female anger, are we taking too much for granted about its value? What if we could make space for both anger and a reckoning with its price?

In her seminal 1981 essay, "The Uses of Anger," Audre Lorde weighs the value of anger differently than Nussbaum: not in terms of retribution, but in terms of connection and survival. It's not just a by-product of systemic evils, she argues, but a catalyst for useful discomfort and clearer dialogue. "I have suckled the wolf's lip of anger," she writes, "and I have used it for illumination, laughter, protection, fire in places where there was no light, no food, no sisters, no quarter." Anger isn't just a blaze burning structures to the ground; it also casts a glow, generates heat, and brings bodies into communion. "Every woman has a well-stocked arsenal of anger potentially useful against those oppressions," Lorde writes, "which brought that anger into being."

Confronting my own aversion to anger asked me to shift from seeing it simply as an emotion to be felt, and toward understanding it as a tool to be used: part of a well-stocked arsenal. When I walked in the Women's March in Washington—one body among thousands—the act of marching didn't just mean claiming the right to a voice; it meant publicly declaring my resolve to use it. I've come to think of anger in similar terms: not as a claiming of victimhood but as an owning of accountability. As I write this essay eight months pregnant, I don't hope that my daughter never gets angry. I hope that she lives in a world that can recognize the ways anger and sadness live together, and the ways rage and responsibility, so often seen as natural enemies, can live together as well.

"Once upon a time / I had enough anger in me to crack crystal," the poet Kiki Petrosino writes in her 2011 poem "At the Teahouse." "I boiled up from bed / in my enormous night-dress, with my lungs full of burning / chrysanthemums." This is a vision of anger as fuel and fire, as a powerful inoculation against passivity, as strange but holy milk suckled from the wolf. This anger is more like an itch than a wound. It demands that something happen. It's my own rage at that faculty meeting, when the voices of students who had become statistics at our fingertips were asked to hush up, to step back into their tidy columns. This anger isn't about deserving. It's about necessity: what needs to boil us out of bed and billow our dresses, what needs to burn in our voices, glowing and fearsome, fully aware of its own heat.

This essay was originally published by the *New York Times Magazine* as "I Used to Insist I Didn't Get Angry. Not Anymore."

The One Emotion Black Women Are Free to Explore

MONET PATRICE THOMAS

In Western culture, anger is red. *To see red* is to be extremely angry. But red is also associated with passion and love. A woman puts on red lipstick before a first date. A child draws a red heart on a white piece of paper and gives it to his mother. Red is allowed its range. First-day period blood. Arizona sunset. The proverbial red flag. And anger, too, is allowed its degrees. But I've learned this is not so for Black women. There are no allowances for our emotions. An angry Black woman, no matter the reason, is thought to have an *attitude*, which is a subcategory of a sub-emotion, a pale orange. This paints us as intractable, unpleasant to be around, and therefore easier to dismiss.

When Black American sons get the talk, the one their parents can only hope will save their lives from state-sanctioned murder by police or any other level of violence or debasement, it is because a Black man's righteous anger is the color of his potential death. Black daughters are taught something, too:

that because we are Black and female in America we must be punished. For Black women and girls, our anger doesn't make us dangerous; no, it colors us another way.

I was one of those tall, gangly girls in fifth grade. Corey, who struck me in the nose with her coat sleeve as we stood in the courtyard waiting for the bell to ring, was one of the shortest. My gut reaction was to respond in kind and so I did, swinging one arm out to hit Corey with a lackluster swipe across her face. We were both wearing those puffy jackets of the late nineties and suddenly we were both windmilling our arms and a ring of students had formed around us. When I came back to myself, I was sitting in the detention room. My only injury was a throbbing nose where the first blow had landed. Across the room, Corey looked equally unharmed, and bored. I, on the other hand, was fascinated. I had never been in this room before. This was where exasperated teachers sent very bad students.

My mother, called from work, arrived quickly. As a much smaller child, I'd noticed the way her tone would change when she was in public, the mask she wore. She navigated the outside world with the false pretense of a pleasantly blank expression, but that was not who she was when we were alone, where I knew her as a sharply astute woman who saw through most bullshit. That day when she came to my school was the first time I heard her raise her voice outside of our home. "Suspended?!" she yelled, and I felt alarmed. She explained to me that the school's administrators wanted me to apologize to

Corey for starting the fight or I would be suspended for the rest of the day. But I didn't understand. I had not started the fight, hadn't really known I was fighting until it was over. Why should I apologize for what I hadn't done?

My mother tried to explain to the administrators that I had never been in this kind of trouble before, that I was a good student. But they were adamant that letting me go would be sending the wrong message; the underlying reason was that Black students were seen as more violent. My mother's back straightened. I was suspended and we left for the day. My mother did not make me apologize for something I hadn't done. And even though I'd made her leave work for the day and had been suspended, she took me to IHOP.

I understood we'd made some kind of stand. Once we were alone, my mother revealed the true red of her anger, cursing under her breath about the school administrators as she cut into her pancakes. And beneath it I felt her sadness, too. She had not wanted me to compromise my values in order to save myself from something worse, but this was our reality. She could not be there to take me for breakfast every time I saw how my anger would taint how people perceived me.

Years later, at a fancy marketing job, I ate a glazed doughnut every morning so I wouldn't bite through my tongue. I laced my two cups of morning coffee with pure white sugar, coating my mouth and hoping, somehow, I could imitate the artificially sweetened tones of my mother. A good friend, a white woman, had recommended me for the job, and on the first day, as I was introduced to the small but swank office of mostly white people, I knew it was her word and not my credentials or interview that had gotten me the position. She'd vouched for me. Though no one ever said so, I was supposed to be grateful to them for allowing me an opportunity, for letting me among them.

After just a couple of weeks, it was obvious that the expectations at this job were absolute perfection and therefore impossible to meet consistently. I worked myself to exhaustion to succeed on one project only to make mistakes on the next, which was unacceptable. My supervisor and her boss sat me down one day in a conference room with the blinds open to people walking to the breakroom. To keep the job, they said with folded hands, I was required to do more, because everyone else around me was doing more—dragging their laptops from the office to home and back again, scraping up instant noodles with plastic forks for lunch every day to get back to their desks quickly.

After a few weeks, I questioned the unhealthy work culture and was put on probation—told I had a month to turn things around. The problem, I thought at first, was me. I'd internalized the messages being conveyed: *Everyone else was capable. Everyone else was doing the work.* But it wasn't true. We were all struggling. Still, the anger I felt had to be put aside, I told myself, because I needed the job. I swallowed their messages of being an outsider, and despite my years of office experience, even my experience as a manager—I wondered if I knew anything at all.

And so, I continued to eat and drink the sweetest things I could find during those hours in front of a screen, ignoring the tingling in my legs and how my vision was blurring, until one day I blinked and blinked and still couldn't see clearly. My work fell behind and my presentations were riddled with errors. Once again, I was pulled into the conference room. This time, I was fired. And my vision cleared. I know what happened to me was psychosomatic—all that sugar and all that anger made my body send out warnings. My vision blurred because I couldn't see myself. I couldn't see that I brought value and expertise to that workplace. I'd missed my chance to take a stand like my mother did all those years ago.

And yet I know that my hesitation to fully express anger or even to stand up for myself has also saved my life more than once. On the night a man pushed his penis into me, just as I was falling asleep, I opened my eyes to look at him; his round face was settled into the stillness of waiting. It was a moment that could've gone on forever it was so incredibly still. We'd left the bar, taken a cab together to his place, and fooled around until, I regretfully assumed, he'd passed out. I'd repeatedly said *I'm not going to have sex with you* before we'd even left, in a way that was both a flirt and a declarative statement. When I felt his weight on top of me, anger spread through me like red wine across a marble floor, but I did not show it. Anger should've been an acceptable emotion to such a violation of the self, and yet I'd had a lifetime of experience that said otherwise.

Womanhood had taught me I was in danger, twofold. I'd gone to his house of my own free will, had taken off my clothes, which he would use to justify his actions. And though I am not a small woman, he outweighed me by at least twenty pounds as he pressed me hard against the bed, so he could easily overpower me. Even mildly under the influence, I knew the best play was to contain what was rising inside of me. To react with the fury I felt may have incited a violent response. As we looked at each other, I calculated how my face should look to make him believe I was absolving him. What was the expression I could conjure that would not encourage him further but that would remove me from harm's way? This is a tightrope many women know. Even today I can't wholly feel the anger his intrusion caused—the unwanted press between my legs, the fear—I think, because if I was angry at anyone it would be myself for being there. And I know that's not right. I know I didn't ask for his behavior. I know that I'd made my desires clear. I know. I know.

White people always want Black women to separate our identities. They want us to choose between our Blackness and our womanhood, as if one is more important than the other. But that night a man violated my body, it didn't matter that we were both Black. And when I worked at that marketing job, it was both my Blackness and my womanhood combined that made me an outsider. It's foolish to believe two different containers hold our identities. I exist as both a woman and a Black person at the same time. The world sees me and treats me as both at the same time.

I was pulled over by a K-9 unit on an empty highway on a cold morning and asked to step out of my vehicle. I can only assume the officer's dog was supposed to smell proof of my guilt, because why else would a cop force a lone woman from her car on a lonely Oklahoma highway at four a.m. for doing five miles per hour over the speed limit? Why else would he direct me to get into the passenger seat of his SUV, where I could feel the warm huff and whine of the German Shepherd against my neck through the metal cage between us? Maybe when I rolled down the window the officer had been surprised he couldn't smell my true crime—existing as a Black woman—and so he needed his dog to confirm his hunch. There was no way I could be guilty of nothing more than speeding.

Sitting there beside him, looking at the pale dome of his head through thinning hair as he ran my license, checked my registration, and questioned why I was driving the car I owned on a public highway, I didn't let myself feel anger. Outside, the sky was still dark. It was late January and another hour until sunrise. I'd been trained for this moment my whole life, since I'd seen my mother calmly explain to the school administrators that I would not apologize for something I hadn't done. I knew to be polite, deferential even. Once again I fixed my face, this time into a picture of innocence. I thought of when a white boyfriend of mine had leaned his arms against a cop's window ledge and "vouched" for my character, getting me out of a much scarier situation with just his word. There was no such help on this day. My indignation, no matter how valid, would not seem like indignation, it would seem like an *attitude*. And for all I knew, an *attitude* could be seen as threatening. This was before bodycams. It would be his word against mine. My anger, like a shaken can of soda, sat still inside me until hours later when I was hundreds of miles away driving through the rich green of Appalachia and it could finally release itself with such force I had to pull over for a second time that day.

When the officer asked why I was driving just outside Oklahoma City so early in the morning, I did not say, "None of your damn business," which is what I wanted to say. Nor did I tell the truth: I'd packed my car with my possessions, including a black cat, and had left my boyfriend, a man I loved. And that even then, in the middle of leaving, even then sitting next to the cop, I was full of regret, but also too stubborn to go back. Instead, I said, "I'm moving home to live with my mother." When I'd called the day before, my mother had not asked why I needed to come home. The reason didn't matter. She'd just wanted me to make the trip from Arizona to North Carolina whole.

I did not expect sympathy from the police officer, and none was given. I'm not sure what I would do now in the same situation. I don't know that I would refuse to get out of my car, or tell the cop I felt unsafe or ask for his badge number. It's easy to look back and see all the missed opportunities to take a stand.

That morning, sitting in that car as that cop's dog smelled my hair for drugs and he wrote me a warning ticket, I survived, and that's all that matters to me now. Just as I survived that job and the man who assaulted me and all the other times fear was the preceding emotion. Because, you see, that's the hook, though it took me a long time to realize it. My anger has always been dismissed or overlooked, because it was superseded by the fear of what I'd lose by expressing it, whether it be my dignity, my safety, or my livelihood.

Fear, I finally understand, is the one emotion Black women are allowed to freely explore.

My Body Is a Sickness Called Anger

LISA MARIE BASILE

The first time my body rages against itself, it's 2009. I'm just out of college, and I have awoken to what feels like an explosion inside my skull. Oh god, it's my eye, I realize. My little studio's two windows become my enemies, pouring intense white light into the room. The light is a dagger. I can't open my eyes, I can't think, I can't do anything but scream, literally.

So I hide in the bathroom, where it's cool and dark and I'm all alone, but the light from the main room streams beneath the door, which is enough to send me into a panic. I get into the bathtub and pull the curtain to further block the light. I try to breathe through and into the pain, but this isn't just any pain, this is skull-exploding torture.

Have I finally been turned into a vampire? I joke to myself. Is this it? As someone who'd written a college thesis on vampires and sexuality, that would be a gift. But this? This isn't my body turning from human to eternal creature. This is a napalm in my eye socket.

I have about $76 in my bank account. Going to a doctor, or an emergency room, would mean money I don't have. No parental support, and no more college insurance. Uber or Lyft don't exist yet, so I can't take a quick and cheap ride anywhere. I end up getting a pricey yellow cab ($25) to the doctor who prescribed contact lenses a few months ago. I wrap a black sweater around my head and sink into the back seat. My heart is pounding.

He sees me for free because I slump into his windowless, gray exam room and weep. My eyes look like two swollen, red balloons. One is much more swollen than the other. Somewhere in there is a pupil, maybe some white of the eye. Somewhere in there is the girl I was before.

"You've just got contact irritation, honey," he says. "That's all." He gives me some steroidal drops, which help immediately (but not totally). "Just don't wear the lenses for a few days."

Sitting in that chair, looking up this friendly doctor in his shoddy glasses shop, decorated in pictures of moody, angular models wearing Prada frames, I just shake my head. It can't be just contact irritation—the deep throb is too intense, the light too painful. And my instincts are leading me. I am a lighthouse to myself. I don't know it yet, but this is my induction into the society of the chronically ill and chronically silenced. This is my first taste of what it's like to have my intuition erased because someone has a degree in medicine and I don't. To be furious with my own body and with the way others look past it.

I stop wearing the contacts, yet every so often my eyes seem to blow up. By autumn of 2010, I start grad school by going into debt and by using a scholarship. I'm getting an MFA in writing, but the excitement is dimmed by thinking of those halogen-lit rooms. The light!

The light and I are no longer friends. I become a creature of the night, which may fit my poetry-writing goth-girl persona, but I never wanted it to be literal. Literal darkness is different from artistic darkness. In the dark, creatures go blind. They don't need their eyesight, so they lose it. I don't want to learn how to live in the dark, not like this.

I Google all the reasons my eyes might be doing this to me. None of the reasons look very good ("oh god I am dying of brain cancer" becomes a regular thought), and a lot have to do with autoimmune illnesses, which I don't have.

Finally, I see an ophthalmologist, someone who specializes in diseases of the eye. I come in with my right eye exploding out of my goddamned head, sobbing in pain, shaking with sleeplessness and terror.

The doctor orders blood work because "There's no reason this should be happening without a greater systemic issue." "I'm twenty-five, I'm normal," I keep whispering. "I'm normal."

The blood work doesn't reveal anything, but they're testing me for sarcoidosis and lymphoma and they're asking me about family history: Does someone have colitis, Crohn's? Does anyone have a neurological disease?

"No," I say. *No, no, no*. And yet again they tell me to stop wearing my contacts. "Take these drops immediately if you get inflammation again," the doctor says. The drops can cause cataracts, but hey, that's the solution.

That's it? I think. That's the answer? I'm just supposed to wait until something much worse happens to convince the doctor that I'm right about my body—and that I'm not histrionic, lying, or exaggerating? I've got some mysterious eye problem that requires drops that only serve to make my eyes worse? And living in daily pain, unable to go to class during flare-ups, and sitting in my house with sunglasses on is my new normal?

Unacceptable.

I begin work on a thesis that largely has to do with being sick. I don't realize it yet, but I've become that girl. The one who keeps making excuses because of the way she feels. The one who brings poems about her eyes to class, and keeps her head down.

I discover that Emily Dickinson likely suffered from inflammation of the eye, too—and I write about it, finding some comfort in this dead femme genius who also suffered like I suffer. And then I remember: Emily Dickinson never left her house. Maybe it wasn't just some sorrowful, hermetic nature. Maybe it just hurt too much. Maybe we like to call Emily crazy without understanding her. According to the Emily Dickinson Museum, "For Dickinson, who feared blindness, prolongation of this illness was agonizing in ways beyond the physical. Her doctor's orders for confinement in dim light, no reading. She described this time as 'prison,' her 'eight months in Siberia.'"

In grad school, I have no one to talk to about my eye pain. I don't know anyone else with mysterious, chronic symptoms and this makes me lonely. At least I have Emily.

My aunt with eye cancer suggests Wills Eye Center in Philadelphia. It's a major hospital with specialists. I tell my doctor I'm going and he scoffs. "You don't need a specialist," he says.

"I want an answer," I say.

"You have iritis. It's caused by an eye injury—probably sticking your finger into your eye too hard when you put contacts in." Since he can't figure out the real issue, it must be my fault.

I gently remind the doctor that I haven't used a drill to insert my contact lenses, and that feeling like absolute shit with two enlarged assholes for eyes just cannot be normal.

"Well, you're not sleeping from the pain," he suggests. "Try to settle down. Relax."

This is the breaking point: I understand now that there are two clearly delineated sides in this war waged against my body. The side that fights for it—me—and the side that doesn't, that says my pain is par for the course and to take it, because it's probably not that big of a deal. The side that wants answers, and the side that suggests it's my fault. The side that wants to be heard, and the side that's not listening.

At Wills Eye Center, they diagnose me with uveitis, an inflammatory condition that destroys the eye tissue, and test me for something called HLA-B27, an antigen associated with certain autoimmune or immune-mediated diseases. They think I've got ankylosing spondylitis, a degenerative, inflammatory spinal disease, which sometimes first presents with uveitis. I test positive, but no radiography can confirm it.

I'm sick, but no expensive, fancy machinery can find out why. To exist in this liminal space—of being sick and unable to prove it, of being in pain but unable to predict it—is wearing on me. I stay up at night wondering if I'm crazy. What's that pain? Why am I so tired? I wonder if, when I tell my friends I've got to go, I'm creating my own prison of sickness. And the pain—it's always present. Soon enough, a day won't go by where my hip or my neck or my back is free from pain. I won't remember a life where the sky is blue and the dinner is delicious and the people are laughing and I'm not standing in the back cracking my back and contorting myself into positions that help relieve the ache. The doctors tell me to come back when the symptoms reappear or worsen. I'm silenced by my doctors and by my own body; it's not sick enough to prove itself right.

Then, for a few years, the uveitis stops. This is a dream come true. I can see, I can go to class, I can work on computers, I can function. My face looks like my own again. But by about 2016, my back starts to hurt constantly, I'm always tired, my joints are wildly swollen, I'm always in the bathroom, and I generally start to prefer staying in to going out. I begin to morph, to grow inward, to worry. My friends get used to me canceling plans; they call me "flaky." I try not to make myself a victim. Am I hypochondriac? I wonder. Am I just a delicate little flower?

Something is wrong, my gut says.

During a summer vacation in Italy, I crawl into a silent, candlelit Catholic church atop a small island in the North. I'd been walking all day, through the lush gardens and palaces of Isola Pescatori and Isola Bella, off the coast of Stresa in Lago Maggiore.

I'm not Catholic anymore, but my bones are hurting, and a part of me takes solace on a pew and in the sacred, echoing rooms. I find the coolness comforting. I'm alone but for one or two tourists standing in the back, applying holy water from a font. I walk over to it, dip my fingers into the water, and smooth it across myself in the shape of a cross. I am so worn down. My back is on fire. My fatigue is my albatross. And it hurts to accept it. How does one go about accepting their own limitation? In a sense, leaving my demise up to fate—cancer, a car accident, choking on a plum's pit sometime in the future—felt manageable. But to think that I'm thirty, I'm in constant pain and can't do the things I used to do, and that this may be life? That thought is like a death sentence. A dark, empty hole that lingers above my head.

I am so weary I seek solace in a god I no longer believe in. In this moment, I know that life cannot go on being the same. I am tired. I am a tired girl. I am an in-pain person. I am different now.

I have morphed into a thing that needs comfort, a thing that needs softness and breaks and time.

I am angry and resentful of friends and family who can't see it. Of them not noticing how tired I am. Of them telling me "Well, you look okay to me." Of them telling me to do yoga and drink green juices and meditate. Of them telling me it's the eggs we eat. It's the meat. Gluten. It's pollution. It's my job.

As if I have a choice in most of this. As if I have the time or money or energy to fill my days with yoga and juices and swims and stress-free, vegan lunches. I learn then that everyone wants to be your doctor, but no one wants to sit down and talk to you, face-to-face, about your past, your symptoms, or what you've tried before. They say things like, "Have you tried turmeric," "I have a great acupuncturist," or "This is a spiritual awakening!" What they mean is, "I care," but how it's translated is usually, "My quick fix could end your suffering." These offers to help sound flippant and trite—no matter how lovingly they might be intended—as if a smoke cleansing ceremony is going to magically undo the body's attack against itself. In the end, the issue isn't just other people. It's who you turn into. It's the loneliness of being sick. It corrupts even love, even kindness, and it reduces your patience to ash. No one wants to carry that.

The final diagnosis comes in 2017. I'm at the fanciest hospital in New York City, paying hundreds of dollars to get a fucking answer. I remember what the doctors said years ago, that they thought I had ankylosing spondylitis but had no proof of it.

I want proof. And I get it. I demand it. "You have ankylosing spondylitis," the rheumatologist says. My X-ray shows it this time. My spine is fusing.

"Start the immunosuppressant," he says, still typing on the computer. "You'll inject every two weeks, right into your stomach or butt."

I think, Look at me in my eyes.

"What?" I say. "Every two weeks? What is this medication?"

"It's the best on the market."

And with that, he's done. He's rushing me off, compassionless, ready for the next number.

"Let me know when you're ready. We'll show you how to self-inject and get you your kit."

What he doesn't mention is that the medicine causes cancer, that it doesn't actually guarantee progression prevention. That some people get sick when taking it.

The medicine hurts, and none of my friends know how to ask me about it. They either don't understand that I need a medicine for an invisible illness, or they assume the medicine is fixing me when it is not. My immune system shuts off completely and I get shingles and a lung infection. I stop the medication. The cycle continues: different drugs, different physical therapies, holistic treatments, self-care like it's going out of style, saying no to plans, pushing through pain, constant exhaustion, the fear that I'll be immobile in ten years. My spine, waging a war against itself—and me. Throughout, doctors telling me to take it easy, that it could be worse, that men tend to experience ankylosing spondylitis pain more intensely than women.

According to the journal *Pain*, there is a real connection between expressions of anger and chronic pain, specifically lower back pain. No shit, right? We don't exactly need science to tell us this. Anecdotally, plenty of women express feeling anger around chronic pain. It's not just the pain that causes it, though, it's that the world isn't built to accommodate invisible illness.

The chronically ill are sometimes accused of "playing the victim" for pity or attention. But if being a "victim" is what it takes to find accommodation, understanding, compassion, financial aid, and employment considerations, sure—I'll play the victim.

In an October 2015 piece in *The Atlantic*, "How Doctors Take Women's Pain Less Seriously," Joe Fassler, on his wife's experience being ignored for hours in the emergency room, writes, "Nationwide, men wait an average of 49 minutes before receiving an analgesic for acute abdominal pain. Women wait an average of 65 minutes."

There's also the 2001 study "The Girl Who Cried Pain," which asserts that when women are eventually treated, they're less likely to receive pain medicine—and more likely to receive sedation, as if we're not in pain, we're hysterical. As if it's not physical, it's psychosomatic. There are cases upon cases of women suffering from chronic illnesses or other diseases—like fibromyalgia or endometriosis, as just two examples—who are told they're either lying or falsely reporting their pain. All of this is compounded for women of color and fat women.

History has drawn women in the shape of weakness. In the shape of melodrama. In the shape of less-than.

My own friends accuse me of "taking it too far." When I cancel plans, I'm a flake. When I leave early, I'm a downer. When I say it hurts, they say, "Well, you look fine." When I say I feel tired, they say, "Well, you wrote a book! It can't be that bad."

I'm convinced we are not trained to communicate with empathy. Instead, we're trained to see sick people as burdens—on society and on our patience and comfort.

How do you not internalize this negligence? How do you fight against this demand for proof? How do you not learn to question the severity of your own pain at every turn? I think of how my doctors seemed shocked I wanted to see a specialist. I think of how my symptoms weren't carefully considered—but instead seen as a fault of my own, as if I wasn't sick but instead guilty of jamming a contact lens into my eye. It wasn't easy to ask for another appointment, to advocate for myself, to demand more blood work. The truth is, if the pain wasn't as severe as it was, I may have just cowered and ignored my instincts. I may have just accepted that I was being paranoid, hysterical, overly sensitive. Why does it take so much to make them see?

I think of my mother, who is on Medicaid—which limits her options for care. She has waited months for an appointment with a thyroid specialist only to be told that she is "not the professional" and just needs to wait for the medicine to work. I think of her stress and frustration, how that stress affects her health, how that stress adds up over a lifetime.

The silencing and the invisibility lead to anger, and the anger leads to sickness. Poverty and ignorant employers lead to anger, and the anger leads to sickness. Insurance bureaucracy and the lack of social and community accommodation lead to anger, and the anger leads to sickness. The whole cycle is broken; the body learns to lean into that constant surge of stress hormones and negativity, and the body stays ill. That's the collateral of a system that erases the voices of the sick and disenfranchised.

I am a spine on fire. I am a collection of joints and bones and tissues that wage war. I am every step in pain. I am not thinking clearly. I am not moving quickly. But I'm also not going quietly. Gone are the days of staying silent when a friend reduces my experience. Gone are the days of sitting idly by when a doctor refuses to go into detail. Gone are the days when I snuff out my light simply so others won't feel the glare. There is too much beauty in being alive to silence my intuition, to ignore my body, to not sing its needs and demand that they be met. As it turns out, my anger has become my savior.

Rebel Girl

MELISSA FEBOS

My father and I sat in near silence for the four-hour drive to western Massachusetts. The worst possible thing had happened: my father had read my diary. Now, my parents were sending me to summer camp for three weeks. Over the previous eighteen months, I had undergone a personality transformation. They had seen the outward signs—how my grades slipped and my once gregarious and sweet disposition now alternated between despondency, sulking, and fury. The diary revealed that this new me also lied and drank and spent as much time as possible in the company of bad influences and older boys who either believed that I really was sixteen or didn't care that I was actually thirteen. I, too, was confounded by my transformation and so my diary offered a meticulous accounting of events with little reflection. When I imagined my father reading it, my mind blanched white hot, like an exposed negative. My body was brand new but felt singed around the edges, already ruined in some principal way.

As we neared the address of Rowe Camp, our station wagon trundled down a winding dirt road for what felt like an interminable length of time. I desperately wanted to escape my father's company and also loathed the idea of spending the next three weeks at what I imagined would be a grisly tour of compulsory activities as boring as they were wholesome: hiking and campfires and trust falls into the arms of teens who swore they'd never let a cigarette soil their lips.

A bloodcurdling shriek interrupted the silence and startled me out of my sulk. A small band of teens hurtled out of the woods, barefoot in cut-off jeans and little else—their faces and bare skin emblazoned with streaks of paint. They screamed like feral creatures and descended upon the car. One jumped onto the hood, slapping the metal like an ape. Did I scream? It would have been a sensible reaction. A ghoulish face pressed against the passenger side window and growled, "Welcome to CAMP, CAMPER!!!" I recoiled, as fear and excitement spurted in my chest. The window might have been a mirror and I faced with some wild and estranged part of my own psyche in its glass.

Ours was a regular town—on the big side, liberal in a suburban New England sort of way. That is, my neighbors mostly voted blue, but in the tourist economy of Cape Cod, both the rich minority and working-class majority skewed white and culturally conservative. With my Puerto Rican sea captain father and psychotherapist mother, we didn't fit in. If our optics hadn't set us apart, our politics still would have. As a kid in a stroller, I had marched for abortion rights and environmental protections. When I learned to read, I discovered that my mother had corrected all my fairy tale books with a Sharpie so that the female characters were responsible for more of the heroism. My bedtime lullabies were Holly Near songs and my first concert Sweet Honey in the Rock. By thirteen, I'd already won my first literary accolade: a poetry prize for girls from NOW, the National Organization for Women, whose local chapter meetings I had, until recently, attended with my mother and her friends.

The only thing I'd called myself longer than a writer was a feminist. But my feminism was my mother's feminism, second-wave consciousness-raising feminism, Ms. magazine–reading feminism. I had no feminist friends my own age and already knew better than to use the word among my peers. Similarly, I knew that I was queer and that it wasn't safe to admit that at school. I knew about the evils of capitalism and patriarchy and I still had a secret eating disorder. There seemed no way to reconcile these things. When puberty hit, how was I supposed to rebel?

I packed up my nascent political beliefs and shoplifted some skintight bodysuits. I soaked my bangs in Aqua Net and fried them in a curling iron. I lied about my age and let those older boys grope my precociously large breasts. A new heat urged me toward them, a small oven of desire I hadn't known was in me.

Their hands never failed to smother it. Still, the rumors spread at my middle school and soon the girls I'd known since kindergarten called me a slut. Boys who'd played baseball with me on teams coached by my father made crude gestures when I passed them in the hall. Of this torment, I told no one. Least of all my concerned parents. Outwardly, I barely reacted to any of the humiliations that had suddenly become so common, though I burned with self-hatred, as if I'd ingested a poison that was slowly blackening my insides.

At home, I locked the door of my room and let the floor become a cauldron of dirty clothes. When forbidden from sleeping over at my friends' most unsupervised homes, I slammed the door and flung the small precious objects atop my dresser—a glass candle holder, a figurine of a deer—against the wall until they smashed. In discreet moments, I seethed with a particular kind of rage, as marked by shame as it was rebellion. To direct it at my parents was a small and unsatisfying release. I had never felt more alone.

This summer camp was not, as I'd feared, filled with campfires, canoes, and crudely woven friendship bracelets. This camp offered workshops like "existential crises on the back porch," zine-making, and creative writing led by a Nick Cave lookalike named Dave, who gave us Rilke's *Letters to a Young Poet* and said only one sentence all afternoon: "I hate white people."

The camp director that year was a woman named Nadia. In her early twenties, Nadia was six feet tall in combat boots and overalls with a shaved head and arms emblazoned with tattoos. She stomped rather than walked and used the word *fuck* as though it were the interstitial glue that held all other words together. I hadn't known that women like her existed, that her kind of beautiful was an option. When she looked down at me, though terrified, I felt more seen than I'd ever felt under another person's gaze. I have since learned that recognizing the invisible parts of oneself in another person can feel like a radiant kind of love.

I hadn't known until then that there were other kids like me. That is, deeply thinking and feeling. Interested in art and politics. Misfits in the landscape of American normal. I'd never met young men who could talk about their feelings, let alone about the trouble with gender and sexism. Still, they didn't hold a candle to the girls. The girls at camp wore holey jeans and cut the necks out of their T-shirts. They didn't shave their armpits or flatter boys or cringe at the word *feminism*. Their anger didn't manifest like an ingested poison, silently disabling them with symptoms like starvation or self-harm. It was more like a fire to which they were immune but could spread anywhere they touched, perhaps even me. I was a little in love with all of them, but especially Julia, with her pretty round face, her tiny mouth and nose, her cheeks smooth and delicately furred as an apricot. She was the only thirteen-year-old

I'd ever met who was as committed to her future profession as I was to mine, though she planned on being an actor, not a writer. Once, after an uproarious laugh, her gravelly voice intoned, "I hear laughing burns five calories a minute. Am I skinny yet?"

I had met neither the irony nor the earnestness that I encountered at Rowe—it was the first time I'd ever seen anything that resembled my insides on anyone's outsides. It was the first time I recognized what kind of teenager I wanted to be.

A lot of camp traditions embodied the combination of irony and earnestness. On Field Day, all the interested women played a game called Slaughter. We met in a field crowned by cherry trees and Nadia divided us into two teams: shirts and skins—which is to say shirts and bras, sports or otherwise. The object was to get a partially deflated soccer ball into the opposing team's net. Everyone played on their hands and knees and there were no rules except to forbid serious injury, such as, no biting. Fundamentally, it was a freestyle wrestling activity complemented by some exuberant trash talking.

That year, it rained, and as we knelt in the muddy field, hair plastered to our faces and necks, I quickly forgot to worry about how the wet T-shirt clung to my belly. I had always been athletic, but being a strong girl had stopped being a good thing and having big boobs had ruined the pleasure of running bases and swinging a bat. The self-forgetting that exertion required was not safe in the company of my peers back home. But at camp, we growled and yipped like hyenas, clamped each other's torsos between our muddy thighs. I flung that ball into the net and raised my arms in victory. My new friends tackled me like jubilant puppies.

It was the strangest and most wholesome game I'd ever played and probably the most fun I'd ever had in my life. It wasn't erotic, but it wasn't *not* erotic either. It was through Slaughter that I first realized that the erotic need not be sexual. I was starved for touch and so bereft of any source that didn't estrange me further from my own body that their rough and benevolent hands felt like medicine. Afterward, bruised and exhausted, I lay in my bunk, smiling to the dark. I glowed with a happiness that seemed to arise not from my mind but from my body. (Years later, in a different bunk, I would recognize it after I had my first orgasm with another person, a female fellow camper.) I hadn't known that it was possible to feel strong and animal and close to other women, or that I could enjoy my body in ways that had nothing to do with men or what pleased them.

On the first day of camp, I had stared at the massive hand-painted calendar in the dining hall, at a square in the last week of camp. *Co-ed Nude Beach*, it read. I had told myself that it must be a joke. What summer camp would take its teens on a field trip to a co-ed nude beach? To *any* sort of nude beach? This summer camp, as it turned out. All campers could choose to stay at the clothed beach or move on to the gendered nude beaches or to the co-ed nude beach. When Julia asked which beach I planned on attending, I simply laughed. There was nothing I was *less* interested in than being seen naked.

In the days leading up to our trip to Harriman Reservoir (whose nude beach closed in 2002 when the local Vermont governing council voted in a public indecency ordinance), the staff led community conversations about the difference between nudity and sexuality. Before bed, in our cabins, we had group check-ins about body image and shame. By the time that day rolled around on the calendar, a miracle had taken place. I hesitantly signed up for the female nude beach.

It was a perfect day, the sun dappling the water as my friend H'rina and I lay in the sand, sharing headphones through which De La Soul's recently released *Buhloone Mindstate* piped. Not even my own mother had seen me naked since my body had changed, but here we were: tits out, tampon strings trimmed, sunscreen everywhere. My heart pounded as I peeled off my swimsuit, but after a few minutes of curious looking, it felt shockingly normal. Bodies! How weird, but also entirely ordinary. I immediately understood that no one cared about my boobs even a fraction as much I did. What a relief it was.

Shortly after settling on our towels, we noticed the canoe. It drifted close enough to shore for us to see that it was a man aboard and close enough for him to see us, which was obviously the point. As we began to wrap our towels around our bodies, Nadia strode across the sand, her long body rippling with muscles, breasts bouncing as she marched into the water.

"What the fuck are you doing?" she shouted at the inter-loper. If he responded, I didn't hear it. "You need to GET THE FUCK OUT OF HERE RIGHT NOW," she bellowed. His paddle dipped into the water and he glided away hastily. Nadia stood and watched until he was a speck in the middle of the lake. As she waded back to shore, her pubic hair a glistening black diamond below her taut belly, my heart pounded.

"Goddamn fucking pervert men," she cursed as she passed us, and then playfully shook a cascade of droplets from her shorn head onto our sunbaked shoulders. We squealed and laughed, giddy with nerves.

Afterward, I couldn't stop thinking of the way that Nadia had screamed at that man. There was no self-hatred in it, only the righteous fury of a woman who knows she is being wronged. It was the first time I'd ever seen a woman express such anger publicly. Nothing collapsed. No one shut her up. The man just went away. That she had been *naked* while she'd done it was the most unfathomable part. I couldn't imagine a less empow-ered state than that of being seen nude. At thirteen, I believed in the sovereignty of women's bodies, but abstractly. I did not feel free in my own body and freedom was not the experience I had known of it, especially in relation to men. But Nadia's body could not have been mistaken for a liability in that mo-ment. It had actually seemed fundamental to her power, the *instrument* of her power. For the rest of the day I replayed the scene over and over, thrilling silently to it like a song that names a feeling one thought unnamable.

I was so obsessed with music that I'd developed an unpleasant ear condition by wearing my Walkman headphones even while sleeping, but it had always been a private obsession. In rural Cape Cod, I didn't have access to many streams of popular culture outside the mainstream. Camp was where I came to understand music as a cultural shorthand, a way to instantly recognize one's people. In the pre-internet days of music listening, cassette tapes were passed among teenagers like contraband. It was at camp that I first heard the Pixies, Nina Simone, The Ramones, The Cure, and Ani DiFranco—whose albums I would spend months scouring the record store catalogs for until I realized I was misspelling her name.

Like Slaughter and Harriman, Rock 'n' Roll Day was yet another tradition that upended a typical camp activity; in this case, the talent show. All day, teenagers plugged in on a tiny outdoor stage and played covers of their favorite songs. In the years that followed, I would come to recognize that someone always played, "I Wanna Be Sedated," and someone else, "No Woman No Cry." On the eve of my first, Julia handed me a cassette tape.

"What's this?" I asked her.

"Bikini Kill. The song our band is going to play tomorrow."

"Our band? Like, us? On stage?"

"Yeah. You need to memorize the lyrics. You're the singer."

I didn't want to be a rock star, like some of the other camp-ers did. I didn't want to be a movie star, like Julia. I wanted to be a writer, not a performer. Still, I didn't argue. For the next eight hours, I locked myself in the Rec Hall restroom and listened to Kathleen Hanna sing "Feels Blind." I didn't know who the woman bellowing the song was, but listening to her I felt like I had watching Nadia scream at that man. Like I had playing Slaughter. It sounded as though the singer had gath-ered up all the energy it required to hate oneself and disowned it, flung it outside of her in the form of this beautiful noise. I already knew that art was a way to articulate one's loneliness, but I hadn't known it was also a way to articulate anger. Or that the roiling energy inside a woman's body could be used to express her rage instead of poisoning her.

Until I heard my own voice ricocheting off the tiled walls of that bathroom—*what have you taught me, you've taught me fucking nothing*—I hadn't exactly known that I was angry. But those lyrics spewed from me like steam that had finally found an opening. I was furious. At my parents for getting divorced, at my father for reading my diary, at the boys who used my body and the girls who punished me for it, at myself for my own miserable innocence.

On that stage in my torn jeans and borrowed Death to the Pixies T-shirt, I was so nervous that my voice cracked as I murmured, *All the doves that fly past my eyes / have a stickiness to their wings.* I glanced across the stage at Julia in her torn slip and black lipstick. She nodded at me and I kept going—*In the doorway of my demise I stand / encased in the whisper you taught me.* I made it through the first chorus. Then, in the second verse, something happened. I heard my own voice yell into the microphone *If you could see but were always taught / What you saw wasn't fuckin real yeah* and it was so loud and strong that I swelled inside, as if a space had been cleared and some bright light shone through me. After that I didn't stutter and I didn't have to look at Julia or the handful of dirty teenagers who watched us from the grass. I closed my eyes, brought my lips to the cool microphone, and it was better than any boy who'd ever touch me, better than the crack of a ball on the sweet spot, better than slamming a door or smashing something I loved against a wall. It was like carrying a hammer for my whole life and finally realizing what it was good for.

Almost twenty years later, I heard Kathleen Hanna, the lead singer of Bikini Kill, explain how when she was a college student performing feminist spoken word, the writer Kathy Acker had told her that if she wanted her voice to be heard, she should start a band instead.

I didn't want to start a band. But after camp, I started making my own feminist zine and distributing it around my school even after my nicest teacher suggested it might be a sign of mental unrest. I had decided to be a writer because it felt like the only thing I'd ever want to keep doing for the rest of my life. I had recognized it as a place where I could put my sadness, my thoughts, and create an archive of events that I didn't yet comprehend. That was what I understood art to be. Bikini Kill taught me that it was also a place for my anger. That shame was sometimes just energy one had turned against oneself.

Camp didn't fix me. It didn't cure my eating disorder or prevent me from becoming a drug addict or stop me from handing my body over to people who believed its purpose was to please them. But I did ask my mother to help me find a lesbian therapist when I got home. I started telling people that I was queer and found the courage to kiss my best friend the next year. I memorized the Bikini Kill catalog and awoke to a feminist movement that was more mine than my mother's.

I agreed with my teacher that I suffered from mental unrest, but not because anything was wrong with me. My anger was not a rash or an aberration or a failure of any kind. Like that of Bikini Kill or Nadia or Julia, my anger was a reasonable reaction to the experience of growing up in a country that hated women and encouraged women to hate each other. And my art was not only an appropriate public expression of it but a necessary one.

Why We Cry When We're Angry

MARISSA KORBEL

There is a tremor in my upper lip. It quivers, small shifting, plates adjusting. The top lip shimmering, moving my face in uncontrolled waves, unless I clamp my mouth shut, or press my lips together, smiling. An earthquake (also known as a quake, tremor, or temblor) is the shaking of the surface of the earth, resulting from the sudden release of energy in the lithosphere that creates seismic waves.

I remember the burn of pure fury. I can hold moments of it in the tightening of my ribcage, the tingle at the back of my neck. Once, rage lived in the heart of me, once it breathed between my ribs.

When I was nine years old, I kicked Colt Martin in the crotch. He wouldn't leave me alone. I sunk my elementary-school-sized foot into the place where his legs met, and he dropped to the ground. Smell of bark chips and tears.

I got in trouble. The teachers told me I could damage him for life, make it so he couldn't have children. I didn't see the problem. I thought Colt Martin was terrible. I remember this incident like a mantra, like proof that I have lived in a furious body; I have been so mad I wished to split myself apart.

At home I slammed doors, screamed aloud. I pushed my whole weight into walls and floors. I knew how to rage without crying. I knew how to be explosively mad. Until one day I knew I shouldn't do that anymore.

Nobody sat me down and taught me that rage was ugly on a girl. My liberal, West Coast, free-spirited private elementary educators never would have said that I couldn't show anger.

The world taught me that rage was ugly on a girl.

I curated my emotions to look the way they were supposed to: pretty. My anger pacifiable, easily calmed, all pink cheeks and dainty trembling. A whisper-rage that tremored through me. I wanted to behave. I wanted to fit into the mold of girl. And inside my body, alchemy began: when I got angry, truly, rumbling, seismic angry, I began to cry.

The human body creates three types of tears: basal tears, which keep your eyes lubricated and functional; reflex tears, which are produced in response to a physical stimulus like dust in the eye in order to remove the irritant; and psychic tears, which are emotionally responsive tears. Other animals make the first two kinds; human beings are the only animal known to make psychic tears.

Everything I've learned from the time I was born is essentially some form of control. Basic lessons: how to control my hands, my body. Advanced lessons: how to control my volume, my appearance. Having control over myself allows me to choose. I can present myself as loudly or as softly, as boldly or as meekly, as wildly or as calmly as you wish.

At four years old, I taught myself to cry on command. I remember staring into the mirror in my bedroom, willing myself to cry. It took a long time, endless attempts, until one day, I managed to eke out a tear. I watched it, fat, crocodile, sliding down my cheek.

I had a new control.

My grandfather said that women only cried to get something. I knew some part of that was true: I had cried many times to get something that I wanted, as a device. It gave me a way over the wall of a no. It could be manipulative, but not always. Only when I controlled the flow, and often I did not.

Crying on command was a neat trick, but it was an easy one. The greater challenge, the one I'm still trying to learn, is to stifle tears when I don't want them.

I've learned to warn people ahead of time: sometimes I cry when I'm angry. It's like hiccups, but more infuriating. Sometimes the tears make me angrier than I was before they started. Unwelcome water, flying out of my eyes while my throat clenches harder.

The signal to cry emotional tears comes from the limbic system, the part of the brain that regulates emotion and stores our long- and short-term memories. People cry in response to many emotions, the most obvious one being sadness. But for over half of women, also anger.

I once worked for a man who covered my drafts in red pen. He lashed disapproval on all of my pages. It was a kind of murder. He would call me into his office. I would sit in the leather chair across from his large desk. He would read through the draft I had given him, and he would tell me what he hated about it. He wrote notes like: "Are you sure you went to law school?" in the margins. After, he would hand my draft back, and I would drop my eyes and shuffle out of his office to my desk.

Then: down the hallway, to the bathroom where I wouldn't turn the lights on. Screaming into the crook of my arm. I hated that job, that man. I could never keep myself from crying, sometimes in front of him, and I hated myself for that, too.

I have felt tears streaming from my eyes at the angriest moments of my life: while being critiqued, when my boyfriend and I fought, when my boss told me to "give him a spin." Ear-burning fury in those moments, and also, wet eyes.

I lack control.

Whether produced in response to pain, sadness, or anger, the mechanism of emotional tears is the same. The lacrimal gland, located between the eyelid and the eyeball, creates the tear.

The eyelid blinks reflexively and spreads the tear across the eye, creating a film. The tear is then channeled into the lacrimal punctum (a small drain that empties into the nose, which also explains why your nose runs when you cry). When the volume of the tears overwhelms the drain, tears spill over the bottom lid and down the cheek. That is the anatomy of crying.

The problem with rage tears is that they're not composed. They are decomposition, falling apart. I do not know how to unleash what's in my throat some days, and I do not know how to keep it all inside. At the earth's surface, earthquakes manifest themselves by shaking and displacing or disrupting the ground.

Things that have made me cry in rage: waiting for late people; traffic; mansplaining; cleaning my room; getting my period; kissing a boy that I didn't want to kiss because I didn't know how to get out of it; broken mirrors; spilled breastmilk; my mother's derision; my partner's stubbornness; lines in supermarkets; the NICU nurse who threatened to keep my daughter; my broken foot; parenting; the 2016 election; my father; my best friend kissing my ex-boyfriend; hunger.

While over 51 percent of women have experienced angry tears, under 2 percent of men have. Even as crying has become more socially acceptable for men, it is only acceptable in response to sadness or pain. When angry, men are much more likely to act out physically in aggressive ways. Women are more likely to cry.

I asked on social media about rage tears. Almost every response I received was from a woman. Some of them talked about their shame in not being able to control themselves, in looking weak, in losing their power in an argument. One woman said she thought of them as a decelerator, something that kept her from going all the way off. Almost every woman said their rage tears made them avoid arguments or leave them once the tears came. Many, many women mentioned having to deal with their rage tears in professional settings. Crying at work is practically outlawed in employee handbooks. The film-maker Deborah Kampmeier said that she'd recently embraced the power of her rage tears. "They can blow everyone out of a room if necessary." I loved her regal take on what feels to me like an impossibly girlish problem.

One study suggested that women's tears carry a scent that slows testosterone production in men, deescalates aggression, and kills their sexual response. The limbic system is the same place that *fight, flight, freeze, appease* comes from. It is the part of us wired for survival. Does crying help women survive?

"Depression is rage internalized," my second therapist told me. I had squelched and winnowed and edited my rage down to something that looked like sadness. Something that didn't shimmer like anger, but glistened with a dull, flat endlessness. I had stuck my burning so deep that I couldn't feel it, not for years. I had to go down into the dark of me, where I'd shoved rage, and call her back up. I entered the labyrinth, walked without string. And when I found her, I let her breathe.

I recovered my fury and I found my writing voice at the same time. You could say rage is the root of everything I've ever written. Rage is the fuel of my voice. Now I'm afraid to be soft. I'm afraid to stop yelling. I'm only comfortable growing hot behind the ears, prickling.

I still cry all the time.

My top lip vibrates. I clamp the lower in my teeth. Left side, small bite, a malformed pillow of pink flesh curling right. I dig my incisor into the fleshy bottom lip. I swallow the furious ball in my throat, but it does not go down. I feel like an electric line, snapped from the pole by the wind. A live wire. I spark against the ground.

Earthquake size ranges from those that are so weak they cannot be felt to those violent enough to toss people around and destroy whole cities.

I want to light the trees on fire with my eyes. I begged for powerful, to have some magic in me. I wanted to lift a house with my fury. I wanted a heart full of vengeance, but what I got was a handful of tears.

But crying is our first language; it is the original sound. Before we know words and their meanings, before we know consonants from vowels, a book from a ball. Before the before, on the first exhale, we cry. Lidia Yuknavitch says that crying is articulate, it is language. Then we have narrowed the language of the body, the ways we speak without words. Not all tears are sadness. Not all rage is yelling. Sometimes the wires between one thing and another get crossed, synaptic fizzles. Sometimes it comes out as a sigh, or a thud, or a whimper. Sometimes it looks like tears and tastes like fury.

On Transfeminine Anger

SAMANTHA RIEDEL

I was about five years old the first time I wore a dress. Bored and eager for companionship with the girls who lived across the street, I gamely agreed to toss on a frilly, black-sequined monstrosity—the sort of thing you'd dress a baby princess's corpse in for her untimely funeral. After hearing their shrieks of laughter, I certainly *wanted* to die. Running away, uncomfortably aware of how pleasant the dress felt around my hips, I resolved that this would be my most carefully guarded secret, never to be shared with anyone.

Not long after this adventure, my parents noticed something different about me: I was becoming a bully. After multiple incidents of fighting, I was caught in the coat closet with a henchman shoving a classmate back and forth. Steaming with fury, my father made a rare visit to the school to take me home. In the car, he gave me an ultimatum: explain why I was acting out, or he'd give me a spanking I'd never forget.

The problem was, I had no idea why I'd been doing the things I did. Terrified and ashamed, I sat in silence the entire ride and received a thorough lashing with Dad's leather, buffalo-nickel-studded belt when we got home—a beating that, true to his word, still makes me cringe today. It completely destroyed what little emotional communication I shared with my father, and we never spoke of that day again.

By the time I figured out why I'd acted so aggressively, my father was dead, and I would never get to share with him the truth: I was transgender—a girl who didn't understand how to be herself; a girl who tried to perform masculinity in the only ways she knew how, through violence and aggression; a girl who would grow into a woman who knew the power of anger and how to wield it.

Despite not actually wanting to be a boy, I spent my middle school years desperately trying to figure out how to be one. Bands like Weezer and Green Day, fronted by sensitive but angry boys who railed against everything from the Iraq War to the injustice of getting rejected by cute girls, became my fascination. I read Batman comics and their myriad stories of one man's eternal fury, turned to noble ends in the war on crime. Somewhere therein lay the answer, I was sure; I just needed to put together the pieces to find the kind of masculinity I needed to perform.

I wasn't just trying to be a boy for myself, though; I learned to replicate masculinity for safety. At recess, boys who I considered friends would often steal some possession of mine (usually a lunch box) and play a rousing game of keep-away. I quickly learned that while tears and pleading only exacerbated the problem, a performative display of fury backed up by physical aggression would halt the bullying for a few weeks. One weekend, a boy stole my bike for several hours as a joke. That Monday after class, I chased him through the churchyard near our school and tackled him to the ground. My safety was assured for months. This was the learned language of boys.

By the end of high school, I'd figured out how to ape the kind of masculinity I thought I could live with: a soft-hearted punk boy who just happened to harbor a top-secret crossdressing fetish. I scampered off to college and immediately began writing editorials for one of the student newspapers, based entirely on what made me angry that particular week: the Israel-Palestine conflict, misconduct by the school administration, Bristol Palin—everything was up for grabs if it sufficiently stoked my ire. I wrote with passion, fire, and very little self-reflection or research, burying myself instead in the theatrics I thought were essential to my "quirky nerd boy" personality; the administrative council became the "Dark Council," with our president "in her ivory tower" meting out unjust punishments. I was, to put it mildly, A Lot to Deal With.

During this time, my father passed away after a long battle with brain cancer. I sat with him in his last hours, the two of us alone with the lights off in his cold and sterile hospice room, once again unable to find the right words. I couldn't even cry. Emotionally illiterate and wracked with guilt and shame, I turned my anger inward. Someone like me would never experience the happiness I wanted. I didn't deserve it. Instead, I bottled everything up (just like I knew men were supposed to do), graduated from college, and started writing professionally.

Eventually, though, I came to a tipping point. After an extended stretch of unemployment left me with ample time to contemplate my feelings, I had to face up to reality: my depression and emotional self-harm were just symptoms of my larger problem—I wasn't a boy, I didn't want to live as one, and the only way forward for me was to transition.

Mere weeks after I took my first estrogen pill, a transgender woman named Kathy Sal was followed home and beaten so badly she had to be hospitalized. Not long after, a man who lived on my block followed me to the door of my own building and watched until I entered my apartment. I bought a canister of mace on Amazon the next day. All of a sudden, the symptoms of misogyny and patriarchy I'd previously thought of only in academic terms were far too real.

My anger throbbed, and for once, I knew where to put it. Finally, I had a cause beyond aimless self-loathing and liberal talking points: I would return to essay writing and skewer the forces of misogyny and transphobia wherever they flapped their tongues. I emailed an old editor friend of my father's, who eagerly took me up on my pitch for a weekly column about transgender life and politics, which I wrote for a year after beginning hormones.

My early essays, unfortunately, were still reflections of that "boy" I had been in college, who I was trying with limited success to leave behind. My words were thunderous, needlessly combative and unkind—when a band behaved rudely to my friends at a set in the Bowery, I wrote an extra edition of the column to call them "generically wimpy." But it wasn't just strangers who became targets. After a heated exchange about tone policing on Facebook, a cisgender friend continued to push my buttons through text; I responded by writing an entire essay called "How to Be an Ally," using him as an example of what *not* to do.

Finally, two of my best friends (one, my recent ex; the other, a mutual friend who'd taken me shopping for my first dress at H&M) had had enough—but they expressed that in a more helpful way than I had ever considered possible. They invited me over for dinner, poured some wine, and bantered with me for a while, setting me at ease. When the meal was prepared, they told me we needed to talk. "We love you," they said. "But we feel like we can't talk to you anymore without becoming fodder for your next column."

I was shocked and distraught, but I couldn't deny the truth of their words. I found myself crying for one of the first times in years (a definite sign they had gotten through to me, but also that my estrogen was finally doing its job). How could I not have noticed the callousness in my writing? Wasn't I doing this to help people? My anger may have been an effective communication tool, but wielded recklessly, it was hurting and repelling those I cared about. I had been so used to channeling every negative emotion into anger that I had almost missed the opportunity to leave that life behind. My transition didn't need to be a simply physical one; while the hormones reshaped my body, I could unlearn the harmful socialization of my youth and become a kinder, more understanding woman.

By calling me *in* (rather than *out*, as I had been doing to others) that night more than three years ago, my friends helped recenter me in a way for which I can never properly thank them. Although it would be a lie to say I no longer struggle with self-hatred or lashing out, I'm not ruled by those manifestations of anger anymore. I'm forging a new relationship with anger now.

Late one night, I was walking from a friend's place toward the last bus home. Thankfully, it's a short ride, and I wouldn't have to wait long. The streets of Brooklyn were mostly quiet, but as I strolled briskly down the block, I passed a man accosting a woman by a storefront, yelling "you can't" repeatedly as she attempted to escape. My first instinct was to not get involved and keep walking; by now I'd learned exactly how dangerous men can be for people like me. But they can be dangerous for people like her, too.

My bus was approaching. I couldn't make out much of their conversation, but rising above everything else, I heard her voice say, "No."

To hell with the bus. I backtracked quickly.

"Excuse me, is he bothering you?" I asked.

"Yes," she sobbed. *Please,* said her eyes.

The man turned his attention to me, told me to back off, that it was fine.

I didn't, because it wasn't. I sized him up; he was slightly taller than me, but skinnier, and my approach had knocked him off balance. I stepped between them, wondering how quickly I could get the mace out of my purse if I needed it.

"Let her go home," I snapped. His protests meant nothing to me. I felt like I had been training my whole life for this moment. I could tell he was drunk, that he wasn't ready to throw down; his bluster was a bluff, only powerful enough to intimidate one woman—not two, and certainly not one who knows how to hold herself, how to match his anger and not blink. I empathized with her terror, but that night, I did not share it. When I looked into his eyes, it was with all the fury and contempt I felt for the men who had forced me to learn their ways and pretend to be one of them.

I ordered him again to let her go, and she and I stepped away together. Her apartment was only a few blocks away, so I walked her home. We talked like new girlfriends, gushing over how much we loved Brooklyn, glad to have found one another in this vast city. We parted ways, and I flagged down a taxi with the joy of solidarity ringing in my heart.

Deep in the fires of sisterhood, I was reborn.

As a confused trans child, I used my anger as both armor and camouflage—after all, the best defense is a good offense, and lashing out at people seemed like a good way to keep myself from being hurt more deeply than I already had been. But that night, standing between another woman and her abuser, my anger afforded me no protection. I was perhaps more open and exposed than I had ever been in my life, yet I found I didn't need the kind of protection my old anger had afforded me. Instead, I was finding another way to live my most passionate truth.

Trans-exclusionary radical feminists (TERFs), or women who don't believe trans women are really women, would give you a far more chilling interpretation: my propensity for anger and even violence marks me as irrevocably male, a colonizer of women's spaces who has never truly been—and never will be—female.

TERFs believe that because trans women are not often raised as girls, our socialization alienates us from "true" womanhood. I'll admit that on the surface, it seems like they have a point. Repressing a transfeminine identity can hold back emotional development in areas that are culturally constructed as "female," such as the expression of grief or anxiety, in favor of "male" expressions such as channeling those emotions into anger. But all this theorizing falls apart when you try to apply it to cisgender women's lived experiences. There are many women in America and all over the globe whose circumstances require very different socialization; as other marginalized feminists have long pointed out, the concept of a "shared girlhood" is intrinsically false, relying on white- and cis-dominant ideas of how girls are socialized. Women born in areas with high rates of violence, for example, may have fewer issues expressing their own violent anger; in such an environment, repressing such emotions can be a dangerous sign of weakness, while demonstrating strength through fury acts as a powerful deterrent. Does that make them male?

Contrary to TERFs' assertions that trans women pose a threat to cis women and their spaces, I believe we have much to teach one another. Imagine radically inclusive spaces where inquisitive minds explore both cis and trans femininities, where we can each open ourselves to new possibilities of the self and take the next steps toward our collective liberation. When we fill in the gaps in one another's experiences, what possibilities could we discover? On that night in Brooklyn, I tapped into the past I never wanted and found an expression of solidarity waiting where I least expected it. Did I go through that trauma for a reason? When our anger has both power and temperance, what barriers may we yet demolish?

Smashing walls like these isn't easy, of course. The last four years of my life have often been frightening and strange, filled with confusion over my own changing emotions. It's been hard to keep my feet under me. I'm still learning to recognize when I hold onto anger and use it for self-abuse, to let go of that along with nonproductive hostility toward those around me. But the joy of expressing myself authentically is a greater reward than I ever could have dreamed, one that far too many women are still denied. It's time for us to reclaim our anger—and in doing so, redefine ourselves.

Unbought and Unbossed

EVETTE DIONNE

I have always been slow to anger. As a child, sensitivity controlled the way I reacted to criticism. It didn't matter if the person critiquing something I'd done or said used a calm voice or a roaring one. It didn't even matter if I'd done anything at all. As soon as I felt verbally attacked, I curled into myself, hung my head low, and bit back the tears that always threatened to spill onto my chubby cheeks. I was familiar with crying silently in bathrooms and in my bed after all of the lights had been turned off, but rage—the kind that bubbles up and spills over—was foreign. I didn't have the language or the understanding to grasp that there's an intricate relationship between fatness, Blackness, and rage that could make me appear as the aggressor even when I was merely defending myself.

In elementary school, though, I learned that I needed to tread lightly as my body began expanding faster than my peers'. Thanks to prednisone, a steroid prescribed to treat asthma, I grew rapidly between the ages of seven and eight, and more than anything else, I desperately wanted to make myself small enough to be accepted, to be seen but not targeted. Instead of growing angry when children taunted me and doctors spoke about my weight gain as a moral failure, I sank further into myself. When fellow children would touch my hair without my permission and skip me in the lunch line, I just quietly observed, as if their cruelty was happening to someone else.

One day in the fifth grade, however, I snapped. One of my classmates, whose name has long since slipped my mind, was standing behind me in the tetherball line during recess. I had several quarters in my pocket, and when a few of them fell out while I was playing, she put her foot over them, and then proceeded to pick them up.

Ordinarily, I would've pretended I didn't see her pick up the quarters to avoid confrontation, but something deep within urged me to confront her. Anger broiled under my skin, creating a prickly feeling in my hands that still strikes me whenever my emotions get the better of me. When she denied taking the quarters and then refused to return them, I attacked her, putting both of my hands around her neck, cutting off her oxygen, until a teacher saw the scuffle and proceeded to break it up. I realized, in that moment, how fragile her neck was in my hands, and I flushed with shame. How dare I respond to confrontation with violence?

I'll never forget the principal chiding me for physically assaulting someone. "You have to control yourself," he said. "You have to figure out a better way to express your anger."

I heeded his words, and tucked my anger away. I even apologized to the girl I had harmed, though I remember feeling confused about what I was actually sorry for. She'd taken from me. I'd responded. How could I possibly be wrong? I didn't know, at that time, about the educational systems that penalize Black girls, suspending them at six times the rate of white girls, but I knew that my principal wasn't just scolding me for his greater good or to uphold a zero-tolerance school policy. He was offering words of wisdom to a girl already perceived to be older than she was because of the size of her body. It was misguided wisdom, but wisdom nonetheless.

After that encounter, I worried about perception. I was concerned about being seen as aggressive and uncontrollable. I learned in that moment that, no matter how I was provoked, anger wasn't a reasonable response to mistreatment. That lesson has lingered for more than twenty years, as I've gotten older and fatter and more aware of how the world understands fat Black bodies. When you inhabit a body as large as mine, there's a harmful assumption that aggression is inherent, and no matter what has happened, the larger person provoked the disagreement and should be the person to deescalate it. When I enter a corporate office or an airplane or any public space, I am consciously mindful of my approach. A smile graces my lips, politeness attaches to every word, and in an effort to show that I am in no way a threat, I over-accommodate. I find myself shrinking, speaking with an inflection in my voice, adding exclamation marks in written communication to push against the idea that my being Black, fat, and woman automatically makes me a threat. In many ways, though these are protective measures, they do not protect me from fatphobia or racism. Instead, by shunning anger, I am allowing transgressions to happen without penalty.

This is one of the many consequences of existing in a society that frames Black women's anger as unjustifiable. The "angry Black woman" trope, like other controlling images, is rooted in the enslavement of Africans, as Patricia Hill Collins explains in her groundbreaking book *Black Feminist Thought: Knowledge, Consciousness, and the Politics of Empowerment.* Through her research, Hill Collins determined that "portraying African-American women as stereotypical mammies, matriarchs, welfare recipients and hot mommas" justifies the oppression of Black women across the intersections of gender, race, and class, and these controlling images were created and then entrenched in everything from policies to media to present social issues like poverty and racism as "natural, normal and inevitable parts of everyday life."

When I first read *Black Feminist Thought* in a graduate course titled after the book, I had what Oprah Winfrey calls an "ah-ha moment." Reading Hill Collins' explanation of the "angry Black woman" trope, which Dr. Rachel A. Griffin calls "crazy" and "domineering" and Johnnetta Cole and Beverly Guy-Sheftall describe as "overbearing, bossy, sharp-tongued, loud-mouthed, controlling and, of course, emasculating," it finally clicked why that principal had encouraged me to apologize: our anger is seen as illegitimate and wielded without discretion, so it becomes easy to overlook, dismiss, and shun us. That was why my anger had been dismissed, my reasoning overlooked, and I was penalized—even though I'd been wronged too.

Pop culture, in particular, has guided the understanding that fat Black women's anger is always illegitimate even while it presents it as the only way we can gain respect. Take, for instance, Mo'Nique's character, Jazmin Biltmore, in the 2006 rom-com *Phat Girlz*. In one telling flashback scene, Biltmore is taunted on the playground by fellow students because "she can't fit through the cafeteria" door, and her cousin, Mia (Joyful Drake), doesn't even attempt to intervene. Her only friends, she monologues, are herself, her diary, and a prayer to God to become thinner—until she decides to physically react. Later, when a classmate calls her a fat bitch in front of her crush, Biltmore pounces, beating the girl up as their peers surround them and cheer her on. In that moment, she's finally seen after being ignored and bullied, reinforcing the idea that violence is the only way she's afforded recognition. Throughout the movie, Biltmore participates in several fights, including a romp at a fast-food restaurant, and each time, she's able to walk away with more dignity than she came into the encounter with. If you're fat, Black, and woman, it's impossible to wrangle anger in a way that both dismisses the "angry Black woman" trope and acknowledges the harm that has been done to you. Instead, we're often reduced to reactionaries, women intent on using the size of our bodies to bully others.

Though Serena Williams is muscular, not fat, she has been penalized and criticized throughout her career for publicly expressing her righteous rage. In her 2018 US Open finals match against Naomi Osaka, umpire Carlos Ramos repeatedly targeted Williams, accused her of illegally receiving coaching from Patrick Mouratoglou, taxed her with a point penalty for breaking her racket, and eventually cost her a game that was crucial to her beating Osaka. Williams' anger was, in every way, justified, especially in light of the years of mistreatment she's faced in the sport of tennis, including being drug tested more than any other woman in the sport, being accused of purposefully building her body to overpower her opponents, and being taunted with racial and sexist slurs. Even when she's right, she's wrong, simply because of the body she inhabits.

It was only in graduate school that anger became more understandable to me, as I delved into the work of Audre Lorde, bell hooks, Patricia Hill Collins, Robin Boylorn, and other Black women who'd decided they had a right to access anger and were intent on both theorizing its importance and deconstructing how rage had become something to be shunned, never to be expressed for fear of being misinterpreted or caricatured. I immersed myself for the first time in hooks' *Killing*

Rage, in which she expresses her understanding that rage is a "necessary aspect of resistance struggle" and "can act as a catalyst inspiring courageous action." I first encountered Audre Lorde's 1981 keynote presentation at the National Women's Studies Association Conference in which she declares that her response to racism is anger, and that no one is served by being afraid of the weight of anger. Lorde was specifically addressing white women scholars who attempted to tone police her when she wanted to foster conversations about racism, but her call to action can't be separated from rage as a Black feminist political project that can and will dismantle oppressive forces.

In the pages of these books and articles and speeches written by Black feminists, I located my own anger, recognized its legitimacy, and began harnessing it in a way that allowed me to show up fully as myself without fear of confrontation. I realized that I'd developed a different relationship with anger during a class discussion of the role Black men play in perpetuating sexism in Black communities. As I began speaking, specifically referencing an interaction I'd had with a Black man online, one of my Black male classmates attempted to interject. "You can't blame all Black men for one Black man's fuck-up," he began, and I felt that familiar tingling in my fingers. In that moment, I knew I had two choices: swallow the anger and keep the peace, or express exactly how I felt.

After reading Lorde and hooks and Boylorn and Griffin and Dr. Brittney Cooper, I knew there was only one true choice.

Before he could continue, I cut him off, feeling the anger rising in my voice. "Don't interrupt me," I said, voice shaky, but certain that I was right. I can't remember all I said, but I know when I was finished, the room was quieter than I'd ever heard it, and I could feel the anger radiating off the walls. I then excused myself, walked to the bathroom, wetted a paper towel, and put it on my face and neck to cool down. It was the first time I'd allowed anger to guide me in an educational setting—and it was one of the most freeing moments of my life. I knew then, as I didn't know in fifth grade, that I could respond angrily, and not apologize for it, because my anger was justified. After I calmed down, I returned to class, and finished the lecture quietly, avoiding the gaze of the man I had rebuked and reflecting on our interaction. At the end of class, as we were leaving the room, he stopped me and told me he didn't agree with me but he respected my perspective. That was all I needed to stay angry in service to my Black feminist ethos.

I've not participated in many physical altercations since that one in elementary school, but I have stopped making myself smaller and allowing people to step over me. Nowhere am I able to do this better than on social media. Whether it's discussing feminism or fatness or politics, I use my voice online to disrupt oppressive narratives about people from marginalized communities. I do this in my work as an editor and as a writer. Anger fuels my fingers and allows me to correct folks who willfully misunderstand the work of social justice.

Shirley Chisholm, the first Black woman elected to Congress and the first to run for president, used "unbought and unbossed" as her political slogan to represent her approach to politics as a community endeavor rather than an individual one. This is best exemplified in her 1972 announcement speech when she said, "I am not the candidate of Black America, although I am Black and proud. I am not the candidate of the women's movement of this country, although I am a woman and I am equally proud of that. I am the candidate of the people of America, and my presence before you now symbolizes a new era in American political history."

She understood, better than anybody, that being unbought and unbossed meant harnessing her anger and unleashing it strategically and in service to a bigger vision. It's representative of the approach that Black women take to politics, to pop culture, to life. When we understand, as Chisholm did, as hooks and Lorde and Hill Collins and so many others theorized, that our anger is our best gift, it allows us to blaze a new path.

It has taken me years to get this, years to accept it, and years to implement it, but being in touch with my anger as a fat Black woman has made me sure of myself. I'm no longer slow to anger. I quickly pivot to it and then use it to fuel my pen. My anger is a salve. Reclaiming anger as a legitimate response to both interpersonal and systemic transgressions is a Black feminist project that I proudly participate in—finally.

Guilty

ERIN KHAR

Along the dark wood walls hung framed diplomas and a large oil painting—an impressionist landscape of blurry purples and blues that made sense if you squinted. I could hear the hum of LA rush hour outside, beyond the parking lot, on a cool October evening in the Valley. The dark brown chesterfield sofa stuck to the back of my thigh. I pulled down the hem of my gray wool uniform skirt. The light blue boxers I wore underneath—as all the girls at my school did—were peeking out. I looked up and saw that Dr. Geoffrey was waiting for me to say something. *What did he ask me?* I felt the hair band tight around my left wrist and removed it, putting my long brown hair up in a top knot.

"I don't really know how to answer that," I said in that fourteen-year-old way as I exhaled. It was at least partially true.

I resumed running my fingers along the edge of my skirt, opening and closing the pleats. I looked up. Dr. Geoffrey had one arm crossed, the other resting on his elbow, his chin in his hand, like he was studying me, like he didn't believe me.

"You mention that you feel guilty a lot," Dr. Geoffrey said.

"I do?" I asked.

"Do you know what all the guilt is really about?" he asked.

"That I've done things I feel guilty about?"

"All that guilt—it's unexpressed anger," he said.

I couldn't respond. His words hung in the air and multiplied and swarmed around me. My face flushed.

"I don't think I'm angry," I said in a whisper.

"You have a right to be angry, Erin. You have that right."

"I have to go to the bathroom," I said.

I quickly got up and walked out the door, across the hall, carrying the bathroom key attached to a large blue disc. I shut the door behind me and closed the latch at the top with my clammy hands. I put my back against the door and slid down, landing cross-legged on my purple Doc Martens. The bathroom spun and swelled. I turned my head and let my cheek rest against the door—telling myself it was a less-gross alternative to the floor—and concentrated on breathing. I shut my eyes and counted.

When I was four, my maternal grandfather died and took my mother with him, leaving me with a ghost. When I missed her—the before mom—I would sneak into her room, open her bottle of Opium perfume, and carefully put some on the back of my hand so I could smell it through the day.

When I was four, the son of a family friend began to touch me, spreading his angry fingers into all parts of me, leaving his anger inside me. I told no one; instead, I let his anger circulate, and I began to hate myself.

When I was four, I fell climbing on a fence at my preschool, and landed on it, right between my legs. I remember the overalls I was wearing, and the red T-shirt. And the air was perfect that day. I bled; I had to pee in a bathtub for a week.

I'd be lying if I said I knew the exact order of these events, but when I was four years old, I was afraid to fall asleep and I'd sit in the corner of my bedroom, in the dark. I'd sit on my hands because I wanted to break things; I wanted to scream. Anger rose up in my chest, an anger that would materialize inside me from some unknown source. I'd collect its heat in fiery gumballs that I'd swallow whole and lock away.

Then the panic attacks came, and anxiety—the type of anxiety that wraps slender arms around you, squeezing tighter and tighter. To make it stop, I'd hold my breath and count. And I'd smell the back of my hand, searching for some trace of my mother's Opium perfume.

I started keeping secrets. I told them to Sai-ee-doe, my imaginary friend who lived in the antique icebox in the corner of our dining room. I'd climb right in there with Sai-ee-doe and tell my secrets and swallow all the bitter until it burned a hole inside of me.

When I was eight, my parents separated, and the remnants of my mother felt weightless, like they'd blow away if I spoke too loudly. Her gray-green eyes looked elsewhere—past me. I felt guilty—guilty that she was left alone with me in that big Spanish house, left alone to take care of me. I didn't want to need her.

I felt heat rise to the surface, just beneath my skin, living in the spaces between the veins and capillaries that pumped all the blood through my body. The heat took my breath, and one day my breath felt like it was never coming back. Around the heat was something I couldn't identify—a feeling that choked me, a shame rising up in my throat, thick and cloying.

On a Saturday afternoon, I sat in my room on my brass twin bed and picked at a scab on my knee. I heard my mother on the phone—upset, muffled, hollow, far away, even though she was just down the hall. Heat rose under my skin, up the back of my neck. My ears burned. I looked at the Laura Ashley wallpaper on my bedroom walls—white with tiny blue flowers that matched my quilt. I felt trapped, stranded on my bed, an island in the center of a room whose walls with tiny blue flowers pressed in.

I locked myself in our upstairs bathroom and opened the medicine cabinet, unsure of what I was looking for. Inside the cabinet, next to the tiny scissors and Betadine and Band-Aids and dental floss was a golden-brown pill bottle. *Darvocet.* My grandmother's name was on it. It was expired. I didn't know what the pills were, but there was an orange label on the bottle with the profile of a man who looked dazed, tiny bubbles and a squiggly line floating in front of his closed eyes. It read, "May cause drowsiness or dizziness." An exit—an exit from the madness and fury and the mercurial breath that wouldn't just settle in my lungs—in a large red pill that made me gag when I swallowed it with water from the bathroom sink in a toothbrush cup.

I returned to my room, returned to the island of my brass bed, and took out the book beneath my pillow—*The World According to Garp*. I had stolen the book from the wall of books in our den. Reading was what I used to turn to when I was anxious, when I couldn't sleep. It wasn't working so well anymore. I flipped through the book, finding the sentences I'd underlined, rereading random passages. After some time had passed, my head began to feel light and heavy at the same time—too heavy to hold up, but containing thousands of tiny bubbles, like the ones on the warning label—that glided and bounced around inside. I shut my eyes, and the heat of anger hovering beneath my skin and the lump of shame caught in my throat lifted, drifting away like lost balloons.

After that day, I started searching the medicine cabinets of family members and friends' parents. Any bottle with a label of a droopy eye or a head swimming with tiny bubbles or a caution against operating heavy machinery would be opened, its contents winnowed.

At thirteen, I was offered heroin for the first time, by my sixteen-year-old boyfriend whom I'd asked for pills. It was an easy decision to make. There was no decision. It was madness and fury transmuted to guilt and unconsciousness.

At fourteen, I stopped using drugs, and my anger radiated from the ends of my fingers and in hot, furious tears and in words that cut through the air like javelins, and I couldn't control where they landed. The anger was a knife I pulled and a chair I threw at my mother and blood on my arms from fingernails dug so deep in an attempt to harness all that rage.

My parents had no choice; they had to notice. I don't remember talking to them about it, but they sent me to therapy with Dr. Geoffrey. I told him I used to dabble with drugs. I told him I'd lied about having a boyfriend, about where I'd been spending my time. I told him that I felt guilty that my mom was stuck with me. I told him how guilty I felt about all of it. But still, I couldn't tell him I was angry; I couldn't let that door open because if I did, the heat below my skin would burn me into nothing.

I sat on the floor of the bathroom, across the hall from Dr. Geoffrey's office, with my eyes closed, my cheek pressed against the disgusting door, counting and breathing. And I felt angry. Angry at him. Angry for suggesting that I had unexpressed anger.

I stood up and walked to the sink, turned the faucet on and let the cool water run on my hands before dabbing water behind my ears and on my neck. I stared back at my reflection in the dull mirror and slapped my cheek hard. I splashed more water on my face, grabbed the key attached to the big blue disc, and returned to Dr. Geoffrey's office, where I told him everything was just fine.

And I bounced, for more than a decade, between anger and heroin. I went from high to unyielding, unwieldy rage and back again, and I couldn't figure out how to stop one without the other.

Lyssa, the Greek goddess of fury and madness, is the daughter of Nyx—Night. She is madness personified. She inflicts insanity on heroes and rabies on dogs. Lyssa makes Heracles crazy, and he murders his wife and children. Lyssa's sisters, also daughters of Night, are the Maniae—they embody crazed frenzy.

Anger in a woman is akin to madness; it felt like madness inside of me, it looked like madness to others.

Maybe if they let us be angry, we wouldn't go mad.

A partial list of things people have called me when I let myself be angry:

irrational
unstable
toxic
scary
in need of help
in need of therapy
in need of a mental hospital
in need of medication

a lunatic
idiotic
paranoid
psychotic
hysterical
nuts
deranged
schizophrenic
demented
crazy
insane
a psycho
a broken dog
a bitch
a cunt

As a girl, I learned to fear my anger. My anger scared my mother. My anger could land me in a mental hospital, they said. My anger became so many iterations of "What is wrong with you?" that the only solution was to push it down deep into that burning hole and let it come out in any other way *but* anger.

As a young woman, I ran from my anger. I ran from it because I thought it would eat me up. I ran from it because I didn't deserve to be angry. I was a bitch and a slut and a liar and a fraud. My anger left shoe prints on a bedroom ceiling when I kicked off an ankle boot in a fit of rage over what I was wearing. My anger left a trail of spiteful words I couldn't take back lashed out at boyfriends and friends. But only when I was sober.

As a junkie, I was a walking apology. *I'm so sorry I've disappointed you. I am so sorry I relapsed. Again. I am so sorry that I lied, that I stole, that I did all the things I said I would never do. I am sorry that I exist to disappoint you, to bring you shame.*

I took my anger and shot it in my arm. I took my anger and snorted it right up my nose. I took my anger and smoked it off a piece of tin foil, and in a crack pipe. I took my anger and carved up my leg with a box cutter. If I just kept shooting, snorting, smoking, I could kill it all away. The hole in me grew, and Lyssa, the Greek goddess of fury and madness, burrowed herself into its borders.

I'd like to tell you that I figured it all out on my own, that when I hit bottom and went to rehab for the second time it all clicked for me. But it didn't. I kept going, kept running, and then I got pregnant, and I decided to have the baby, despite all common sense.

As a pregnant woman, I wasn't glowing and happy and peaceful and beautiful. I was scared and newly sober and unsure and most of all, enraged. I doubted my decision to have that baby every day of my pregnancy and my parents and the father of my child doubted it too.

I'd like to tell you that when I had my son, Atticus, it all went away, that it all fell into place, that I became the mother I never thought I could be, that the anger just sloughed away like dead skin collecting at my feet. That wouldn't be the whole truth. Things did change when I had Atticus. I loved him more than I hated myself. And that love pushed me forward, pushed me toward getting real help. But it didn't happen overnight, and that baby became a boy, and he saw my anger spin off of me at times and look like madness.

But I did get better.

For the past fifteen-plus years—through talk therapy, cognitive behavioral therapy, getting on and staying on a mood stabilizer, developing a spiritual connection, yoga, meditation, finding a center for myself in Judaism, Reiki, and, most importantly, unflinching honesty—I've deciphered what I'm really angry about. That anger was born in my bedroom at the hands of a furious adolescent boy who took his anger and spread it into me through sex and violence. That anger was cultivated because it was unseen by the people I thought would protect me. That anger was nurtured every time it was labeled as inappropriate, an overreaction, as crazy. That anger bloomed every time a man robbed me of agency, by using *authority*, by using the power of physical force over me. That anger, for so long, had nowhere to go but in.

I have learned to walk through my anger. It hasn't killed me. It isn't madness. There are still times when I have thrown my anger around at the wrong targets, when I have slammed the door, screamed "I hate you," thrown the phone, said things I wished I could shove back in my mouth and down my throat into my diaphragm as soon as they came out. But those moments come less and less.

When those moments do come now, when I feel that old heat rise to the surface of my skin, threatening to burn me, I've learned to expel it through simple actions. I get outside and walk west to the edge of the Hudson River or down and around Washington Square Park—taking in the people, the smells, and the sounds of the city, and that fury lifts, one hot molecule at a time.

And I write. I write my way through anger. I use its energy to motivate myself to speak the truth. And the truth is, I made mistakes. And the truth is, I got back up again. I can take that anger and be a voice for others who might be angry, too. When I do that—when I take all that fuel that rage brings and finally push it out through writing and speaking the truth—then, I am free. And the truth is, I have a right to be angry.

Hangry Women

ROWAN HISAYO BUCHANAN

Many years ago, I watched my mother arrange a bite of chicken, a spoonful of rice, and a curling green leaf on a small plate. It was not for me, or my brother, or my grandmother, or even for her. It was for the ancestors. My Sesame Street–themed chopsticks were not to be touched until she'd arranged their meal.

I'm hungry, I said.

Wait, she replied.

Why? I asked.

The relatives eat first, she said.

My mother explained that after they die, our family members hover around us, protecting us and keeping away bad spirits. But an unfed spirit becomes a hungry ghost. And a hungry ghost is an angry ghost. It brings bad luck. My stomach hurt. My head hurt. I was getting grumpy. It was easy to imagine ghosts whooshing around the apartment, unable to feed themselves, bellies heavy with ache.

I've always been a hungry person and a hangry person. My friends and family joke about it. When I ask when we're eating lunch, they pretend to fear for their lives. It's not that I eat a lot. But I eat often. Always breakfast, snack at eleven, lunch at midday, snack in the afternoon, early dinner. Writing this, I feel the twitches of hunger, the desire to grab an apple or to make coffee softened with soymilk. I hate late dinners. If someone suggests we grab dinner at eight, I'll text back, *Oh wonderful!* All the while knowing that the hours before will be noisy with rage and stomach scrabbling.

The word *hangry,* a mash-up of *hungry* and *angry,* entered the Oxford English Dictionary in 2018. It's a goofy word, one that lends itself to jokes. *Buzzfeed* hosts articles like "The 25 All-Too-Real Stages of Going from Hungry to Hangry" and "21 Things Every Hangry Person Has Secretly Done." And "When You're a Girl Who Loves Food."

At a wedding, I overheard two men talk about how the women in their families become monsters when hangry. It would have been easy to join in. I was raised by a hangry woman. A woman whose hanger built and built until she refused to eat, said she didn't even want dinner, threw her portion of noodles on our plates, or stormed out of the kitchen. I went through a phase of keeping a small chocolate in my bag to offer her, just in case. She'd laugh as I handed over the morsel, and I felt like I'd discovered a grand new medicine.

But listening to the men, I realized it was always women I heard described as hangry. I put "hangry girlfriend" into Google and got 8,740 results. I put in "hangry boyfriend" and got 271. I tried with sister and brother, wife and husband, women and men, girl and boy. The results always skewed female. So, are women hangrier than men?

I live in a bubble. It's a left-leaning, book-loving bubble—the sort of bubble in which it is taken for granted that you believe in evolution, global warming, and the equality of the sexes. I wondered whether in such a bubble the numbers would skew the same way. I ran a poll on Twitter, asking, *Do you get hangry?* I received 139 responses: 81 percent of the women said they do, and only 63 percent of the men. Why the disparity? I was puzzled.

In a 2018 interview with the BBC, Sophie Medlin, lecturer in nutrition and dietetics at Kings College London, explained that both hunger and anger release cortisol and adrenaline. This is why hunger and anger may create similar or overlapping mental responses. But she said there was no reliable evidence that women were hangrier than men. In fact, "biochemically, in terms of neurology, men are much more likely to experience it than women." That makes it even more puzzling that women seem more likely to be perceived as hangry, and even to see themselves that way.

It could be that female emotion is often ascribed to biology rather than rationality. If you can blame a woman's critiques of you on PMS, it's easy to ignore her point of view. The line of thinking that equates ovaries with excessive emotion goes back a long way. The Greeks thought the womb wandered around the body, making women hysterical. Is hanger just another dismissive label for women's rage? A modern-day hysteria, another way to say, "Silly little person, you think with your body and not with you brain?"

Or perhaps we over-encourage men to believe their own rationalizations for negative feelings. In our society, a man's rage is often perceived as a sign of power, while a woman's is a sign of unlikability and irrationality. Maybe men are hangry, but society sees their anger as objectively justified. I don't offer my father a chocolate bar when his eyebrows go down and he gets gruff. Maybe I should try.

Or maybe there are more hangry women because there are more hungry women. Growing up, every girl I knew wanted to be thin. One day, the girls in my year lay on their backs to compare stomach bump height. Did you slope in or out? Were your hip bones sharp peaks or foothills to the mountain of your belly? I imagine us now—our school shirts rolled up, our skin intermittently pimpled, our bodies still growing and sprouting. It would be easy to think this scene ridiculous. But we weren't simply silly girls. Just as good school grades meant good universities meant good jobs, being thin meant being pretty meant being loved. To not eat was a sensible effort toward the goal of quieting the ache for affection.

Magazines were passed around with their top tips. *Don't eat carbs. Don't eat fat. Don't eat in the evening.* Worst of all—*Stop eating before you're full.* I don't know how many girls in that school were hungry. I don't know how many of you reading this essay are hungry. If you are, does it make it harder to concentrate? Does it make it harder to smile? Where do you hold that tension in your body?

Back in school, I wished I didn't have to eat. But if I didn't eat, I wanted to break faces with bricks. I wanted to throw my laptop on the floor. I wanted to bite down on my own arm until I tasted blood. I got spacey and fractious. It was hard to concentrate on homework or make polite conversation.

I tried to figure out a way around the hanger. I realized that when you sleep, no one complains about your mood. It wouldn't matter if I was angry. When you sleep, no one calls you a bitch. And so, I took to going to bed hungry. I figured that in the dark my hanger would not matter. I, with my easy access to food, had been given so much, but I curled up around a ball of ache.

And yes, I got thinner. I woke up early, feeling lighter. I also had nightmares. But there are many reasons for shapes to come from the dark, so I kept going to bed hungry and kept losing weight. I never got as thin as I longed to, because I needed to eat during the day. It took years, but sitting down to write this essay, I am finally grateful for the teenage hanger that forced me to eat.

I have a friend who was an activist. She grew up in a family of immigrants. She was always arguing for the rights of those with less than herself. She was studying global health, but these days she has to leave marches early, her body collapses under the strain. She loved food. Beautiful meals appeared on her social media. She helped organize dumpling parties, made kimchi and chicken. And yet I found myself beside her hospital bed. The papery gown revealed the jut of bone under skin. By not eating, she was destroying her body. She loved food, but she wouldn't let herself consume it.

According to the National Association of Anorexia Nervosa and Associated Disorders, every sixty-two minutes at least one person dies as a direct result of an eating disorder. More women than men suffer from anorexia, although male anorexia may be underreported and underdiagnosed. After all, we associate the illness with women. Starving is apparently a female art.

There is so much famine in the world, while food rots on shelves in wealthy suburbs. If even women under nice cotton sheets cannot be full, it speaks of sickness. If these women are tired, strung out, and collapsing, then the potential they had to do good and useful things slips away. And if we hold up these bone-thin women as the ideal of even a prosperous country, then what future are we selling?

I think of the hangry ghosts. I think of the dead with no family to feed them. Of an eternal hunger, as they watch the living stuff their faces. When I imagine these ghosts, they have the same pained expression I have seen so many women give the bread basket hovering in the middle of the table. Unlike my friend, hunger never carried me to the hospital. Sometimes, at my worst and most foolish, most self-loathing moments, I envy her self-control. Then I realize that that is nonsense and I am filled with another rage. A rage that I know so few women at peace with their bodies. A rage that we tell little girls the door to love is so narrow that they must starve to fit through.

We put only the thinnest women on our brochures, magazines, movies, book covers. This might not seem like that big a deal, but when we put someone in a movie or a magazine we are asking viewers or readers to empathize with that person. We are asking them to feel for her. When we put only thin women in those places, we are saying that only thin women deserve empathy. Not all women feel the media pressure in the same way. Some ignore it. Some feel it and learn to hate their bodies but still succeed in eating. And sometimes, if a woman is feeling vulnerable and scared and unsure of herself, if part of her longs for empathy, then it becomes easy to believe that she must whittle herself away.

I am angry, too, when those starving women, with their calcium-deprived bones, are mocked as vapid. These women are not bimbos or bunny rabbits. They live in a world which tells them that to succeed they must erase themselves. Many of the women who don't eat still want to be seen as smart and as serious. They think that to tell anyone they care about thinness would mark them as superficial. These hungry women pretend to love burgers—but just not today. They pretend they ate earlier. I know one woman who took up veganism only so that she could eat less. I know another who orders huge meals and moves them around her plate.

A few years ago, a doctor found out that I had a condition associated with poor insulin regulation. In a way, it was soothing that something simple was responsible for how upset I got when hungry. Still, I struggle to explain my need to eat. When I say I'm hungry and my partner pets my stomach, something in me clenches—ashamed. There is some part of my brain that tells me that this hunger is weak or sloppy. It takes great effort to push away the thought.

When I think of our collective hunger, I am filled with rage. I am hangry to my heart.

I don't want brilliant, beloved friends to die hungry. Whatever gets me in the end, be it asteroid or global warming or the humble bus—I want to be full. I want to live a full life in the most literal sense. I want that to be okay.

Enojada

RIOS DE LA LUZ

Ghost stories are common in my family. We call each other about any suspected paranormal phenomena in our personal lives. We cleanse our homes and rush into cathedrals looking for signs if we suspect an unusual entity is attaching itself to our children. Some of us pray, others cast spells. We protect ourselves from the invisible monsters in order to face the flesh-and-blood monsters we've encountered.

One of the first ghost stories I heard was about La Llorona, the weeping woman. There are various versions of her story. Sometimes, she's a pregnant teenage girl who is so ashamed she would rather face death than her father. Other times, she's a young woman who promises her firstborn to the church in order to marry the man she loves, but when it comes time to give up the baby, she can't. She runs away with him and soothes him to sleep before she drowns him. There's also a version where she's a beautiful young woman who was born into poverty. She meets a nobleman, who becomes infatuated with her, but they cannot marry because of her class. She becomes his mistress and they have two children together. As time passes, he visits less and less. When she confronts him, it turns out he is to be married to another woman. In her rage, she drags the children to the river and drowns them. Once she realizes what she's done, in desperation, she reaches for her children and treks the water following their limp bodies down the river. She wails for them. Her spirit is said to cry out for them near bodies of water. Children are warned to stay out of the dark water at night so she doesn't confuse them for her own and carry them away.

When I was seven, my chosen body of water was the bath. My heartbeat thudded into the small tub as my head stayed under. Often, I became flooded with anxiety. It crept under my fingernails, so I bit them. It sat on my head, so I scratched at dandruff with my nubby fingers and pulled at my hair, inspecting the curves of the waves. I thought that if I stopped speaking, then none of the secrets I was holding in could spill out.

I was being molested by my mother's boyfriend. He found silent moments in the apartment to creep into my room and wake me. This was my reality for several years. I stayed under the tub water until I couldn't breathe. In the stale water, I held my hands around my neck, asking god or any spirits in the vicinity what I needed to do to get rid of the bad man. As I lifted my body out of the water, I held in my crying, to the point of gagging. I didn't want anyone in the apartment to hear how loud my rage could be.

I don't know what my mother was running from, but she moved us from apartment to apartment when I was a child. I attended over ten elementary schools from the ages of six to nine. The bad man followed us to each new place, much like a demon attaching itself. One afternoon, someone banged on our door with fury. It didn't stop until my mother clicked the door ajar. A woman with a fluffy perm screamed at my mother. The woman claimed the bad man as her husband. She tried to shove herself into the apartment looking for him. My mom blocked her from getting in and the woman spat in her face. Questions flew at my mother. *How could you do this to our family? How could you not know he was married?* At this point, my mother and the bad man had two children together. I felt nothing but warmth toward my younger siblings, but I felt sorry for my mom and this woman. I became enraged with them both. They didn't know the monster I knew. They were consumed with this man, as though he were someone holy or special.

There's another ghost story I heard women tell one another on Sundays when they weren't sure where their partners were. It was usually a conversation between my mother and the friends she met at different vaquero nightclubs, about a ghost who preys on men. On nights of the new moon, in a tight white dress with a long V down her back, she sits by bodies of water turned away from any man who happens to see her. Her hair is long and dark, and sometimes she combs it with a golden brush, other times she just sits and waits. She lures unfaithful men in with the beauty of her figure. As the unfaithful man approaches and asks her for her name, or interrupts her while she's combing through her hair, she turns around and reveals that she has the head of a horse. Men become so petrified, they die on the spot of a heart attack or they have mental break-downs. The women sipped coffee and giggled at the thought of unfaithful men getting what they deserved.

When the anxiety attacks came, I hid in closets and cried in silence until I could feel the embrace of hanging shirts and the smell of sweaty shoes. I imagined myself in a cave scavenging for ancient insects, following them into cracks of the earth. I calmed myself through my imagination. I made up a world full of animals and plants that communicated with me until I could catch onto my breath and feel where my feet began and where my head seemed to be floating off to. I created different rooms where I was safe.

My dreams shoved me into dim rooms with water trickling in the background. I could hear the ocean outside, but there were never windows to escape out of. My anxiety filled me with dread. I had fantasies where I threw the bad man from the second story into the pool in the center of the apartment complex, or I kicked him so hard I could hear his bones break. Anger continued to cycle through me in my anxiety attacks. The crying I held in shook my entire body. I never spoke the truth because the bad man warned me to stay quiet. He said my mother would become upset with us, as though I was a willing participant.

Common stories I heard as a kid were about the devil. As a way to scare us into behaving, we were told the devil lurked in corners and in darkness. The devil grabbed the feet of children who never listened to their parents and dragged them into the soil. The devil left scratches on children as a warning. The devil shook beds like little earthquakes to wake kids up and make them think about the consequences of their actions.

I think it was the buildup of shame. Every time he went into my room, every time he touched me, every time he dragged me by the foot, every time he crushed my small hands into his, I felt ashamed. The shame stayed, the shame calcified, the shame became a tumor under my tongue. Years of shame didn't kill me, but it became a cloud over my head, jolting me with memories about what I could have done, what I should have done, even as a child.

I was exhausted with the panic and the hiding and the silence. He was drunk and walking crooked. I could hear him getting closer and closer. He crawled toward my bed and I could feel his fingers reaching underneath my back. Something electric took over my body, a little voice whispering "no more." I kicked with a rush of adrenaline. I kicked him in the eye and he screamed. The screams of the bad man woke up my cousin. He walked into the room and I launched toward him crying, "He's touching me where he's not supposed to." That's all I could say. The relief in my chest turned back into a boulder as soon as my mother walked through the door. I repeated the same thing to her and she looked over at the bad man. She asked him if it was true. He shook his head signaling no. My mother looked me in the eye and told me to go to bed.

I don't know if I can explain how angry it makes you when someone takes and takes from you only to leave behind panic attacks, uncontrollable fear, and an empty body. A ghost. Rage was as natural as breathing. My panic turned into fear turned into weeping turned into screaming. I boiled over into a mourning teenager. After sexual abuse, you have to mourn for yourself. Oftentimes, no one else will. Sexuality was a warped, terrifying concept. My body was a flotation device. I was a cowering brown body, enraged with what had happened to me. I wanted revenge. I wanted to face him and scream at him. I wanted to break him in half. I wanted to humiliate him in front of his family. I wanted everyone to know what he really was. A thin, molding film stuck to my skin. Bile came up my throat when I froze in panic. I was never scared when I became overwhelmed with rage. It calmed me. It calmed me to think that there was space in my head to see bits of his destruction. I was not afraid of where my imagination took me. I embraced it and started writing.

We arrived home to find water trickling from under our apartment door. My mother opened the door to the bad man sleeping on the living room floor with water flooding the entire apartment. I ran through each room looking for ghosts. I wondered if La Llorona was sending me a sign. She was ready to take me away. Or maybe sea creatures could take me into the depths of their homes. Or maybe it was the horse woman. She was ready to take the bad man.

My mother turned off the sink faucet and tried to shake him awake. She dragged him outside and he finally woke up. I watched as she embraced him in her arms, telling him it was okay, she would clean everything up. My mother cleaned out the apartment day after day and told us of all the things she lost in the man-made flooding. She lost her stamp collection. She lost a bag of photographs. She lost her favorite high heels.

I think my mother understands I will never open up to her. I hear about her through my younger sister. I get the phone calls and the texts. *Mom keeps sharing posts online like "Family is important. Don't wait until it's too late" or "When family goes through life not speaking to one another, the day will come when you regret it. It's called the funeral." Mom said she's looking for your biological father. Mom said she will call you later.*

The first story I ever wrote was a ghost story. The main character, an angry ghost girl, slept on tree branches and attacked lost men wandering through the forest. As a teenager, I turned to poetry. I wrote poem after poem in pencil and watched the callous on my middle finger grow into a round relic. A reminder. I could not undo what happened in my past, but I could write it out of myself, little by little. I wrote about abandonment. I wrote about rage. I wrote about the bad man.

I had not told anyone about the abuse after my mother didn't believe me.

My mother married a Navy man and the family was sent up to Michigan. We lived on an eerie Air Force base and when the time came, we registered for an extremely white school. During orientation, I waited in the school's office for an adviser. A girl with bright blond hair sat next to me. I pushed my body the opposite direction from her. There were plenty of chairs to sit in and there she was. She introduced herself and started talking to me about her trauma. Her accent had a twang in it, but she never told me where she was from. She told me she was sexually abused by her father her entire childhood. She had moved in with her grandmother and was excited to start a new school year in a new place. My name was called and I turned to her and waved goodbye. In Michigan, I made a few friends who listened to the same music. We bonded over eyeliner and goth hearts. I never saw the office girl again. I hoped she was okay. I still do. The office girl sticks with me because of how unashamed she was to tell me her story. She blurted it out without flinching. She struck me as hopeful. I was not at the same point as she in the acceptance of my ghost body, but she made me believe I could reclaim it.

Reclamation takes time. It takes warmth. It takes rage. It takes multiple cleansings. It takes writing under ferocious trances. It takes screaming, even when it feels like no one is listening. It takes scaring those around you with the rage inside your throat. The stories that haunt you, the ones that make you freeze, the ones that were so real but feel like ghosts—tell them without shame. The shame is not yours to carry. The shame is not mine to carry. My body is flesh and guts and dead skin. My body is star stuff and bacteria. My body is mine. My stories are mine to tell and keep. This is my story, in spite of those who tried to take it away.

A Girl, Dancing

NINA ST. PIERRE

I am a girl, dancing.

In shimmering floor-to-ceiling studio mirrors, my leg traced the half moon of *rond de jambe*. My body in *arabesque* was an arrow ready to pierce the sky.

Some days, I felt like a mirage, my life in constant flux. A new apartment, a new city, twice a year, maybe more, as I turned eight, ten, twelve, fourteen. But in each place, Mom found me a studio and I spent three nights a week in class— jazz and ballet first, later modern, hip-hop, lyrical, all paid for by my dad's parents. I danced in show after show, memorized thousands of steps and combinations. It was my home in a sea of uncertainty. My stabilizer. It allowed me to locate myself.

In the studio, my limbs cycled through space in the streaked reflection.

This motion, I could control.

My graduate thesis was the story of my mother's breakdown and death. Toward the end of my program, I met a mentor at a sidewalk café in Philadelphia where we drank gin and tonics. He'd read the three hundred pages I'd written.

"So," he asked, "where is the anger in this story?"

"Anger?" I said. "I don't know. I mean, I don't really get angry."

"What do you mean?"

"Only a few people have ever seen me angry. There was one period when I was younger."

"Yes." He nodded. "And?"

"I don't know," I said. "It didn't matter."

"You have to find the anger again." He tapped the manuscript. "That's where the story is."

I went home and thought about his words: *Find the anger*. I meditated. I moved. The anger was there, I realized. It was all over the pages. It was simply in disguise, performing abstraction or lyricism in some sections, diplomacy and empathy in others. For girls like me, anger was not always wild and red and raging. For girls like me, it was internal decay. It was cool blue, icy islands of flat nothing floating on a cerulean sea.

I am a girl, drinking.

I was sixteen and squished into a booth between my "cool" aunt and uncle at a cruise ship nightclub. The vinyl had warmed to our bodies over hours of B-52s ordered by Aunt

Val. Fueled by the milky shots and many watered-down rum and cokes, I began ranting to my uncle about my dad. I'd asked to borrow $200 from him. He'd said no, but that if I wrote an essay, he would just give me the money.

"A fucking essay!" I yelled drunkenly over the thump of shitty Euro pop.

"Should have written about power dynamics of money." Uncle Kent winked, tipping his Corona toward me.

"That's not the point," I slurred. "I asked him to borrow the money. I didn't want an assignment."

"But, niece, why borrow when you could just have?"

"I know how to work," I yelled. "I've been working since I was thirteen. I needed it for two weeks."

"You're missing the point!" he said.

"No," I said. "I'm not missing the point. He has missed the point. My dad has missed—you're all missing the point!" I yelled, slamming another shot and running onto the dance floor.

"Fuuuuuuck him! Fuck. Him." Hot tears mixed with the sweat streaming down my face, my body slinking and swaying to the bass. Catching a glimpse of myself in the wavy mirrored ceiling, I saw a different dancer. A girl with stunted, short motions, someone trying to stay in the lines. A girl who'd forgotten how to flow. For a second, I thought my chest might split open right there.

No one knew what was going on back home in California. Not really. They didn't know my mother was sinking. That I was in the depths of erasing myself. Ingesting anything offered to dull the pain of a mother I could not mend.

I didn't have the language to tell my father he was concerned about the wrong thing—treating my loan request as a teachable moment on work ethic instead of asking why I'd been crashing with friends and living from the trunk of my '86 Dodge Shadow all summer.

All he knew was that I, a lifelong straight-A student, was on the verge of failing. That I'd missed more than twenty days of school that year. That I was un-wrangleable by my mother, who in turn was inconsolable. She'd kicked me out after I confronted her, but not about the things that really mattered. My lashing against her was petty and violent, a litany of everything she'd ever done wrong—easy to chalk up to typical teen girl rebellion. By then, I was drunk or high everyday anyway, empty booze bottles rattling in the trunk of my car, so she cut me loose.

My father prescribed "tough love" and his go-to, meditation.

And my grandparents, the ones who paid for all those dance classes? They invited me and the rest of my dad's family on a weeklong cruise.

We sipped Dom Perignon on the Caribbean Sea,

I chugged Cuervo in the locker room before first-period geometry.

We watched B-rate magicians in the ship theater,
I drove fast and drunk through the forest, down pitch-dark, windy back roads with my headlights off, staying alive a trick of its own.

We piled our plates high at midnight buffets with ice sculptures of swans,
I smoked opium on dirty bed sheets.

We cracked ten-pound lobsters at a white-sand café in Sint Maarten,
I smoked crack from a tin-foil trough.

It was a stunning display of duality.
When I look back at pictures from that time, I am a ghost, a girl-shell. My normally tan glow a pale, sunken white. My eyes dead in their sockets. But inside I know my stomach was a seething pit, a dormant volcano.

It was around that time I stopped dancing.

I am a girl, drowning.
We were an oversharing, unboundaried, partner-in-crime, spontaneous road-tripping type of mother-daughter duo. The kind you see in indie films and think—if you've never lived that way—it looks mildly thrilling, a bohemian adventure, like

Natalie Portman and Susan Sarandon in *Anywhere but Here*. Except what looks exciting on film is more often, in life, chaotic and destabilizing. Dysfunction has its charms, its free-form perks, but it's only quirky and fun from a distance.

As a poor single mother of two, my mother's life was committed to spiritual growth. We chased nebulous gods up and down California, moving from apartment to hotel to motel to log cabin, praying, chanting, and decreeing, fueled by the slim earnings she gathered from odd teaching and cleaning jobs, welfare checks, and child support.

Enlightenment was her retirement plan.

When I was twelve, she bought a house, settling finally, in deep rural Northern California. I was thrilled to grow some roots. But, slowly, I began to see that maybe all the running we'd done hadn't been in pursuit, but in flight. Maybe the constant motion had rendered the darkness of my mother's psyche fallow.

She started telling a story, a sprawling, slippery narrative about people who wanted to run her out of town, with new characters and subnarratives springing up weekly with little explanation. I wasn't sure what I was more afraid of: my mother's story being true or what it meant about her if it wasn't. If she was capable of inventing the whole thing, it meant that she—my ride-or-die—was a woman unhinged. She would no longer be simply sensitive or intuitive or psychic or spiritual, but mentally ill. And if that was true, what else in our lives had been quilted from thin air?

I nodded along to her daily litany, but slowly, I stopped listening. Behind the scenes, I was cutting my losses, scrambling to craft a contingency plan. Maybe she'd known I would jump ship eventually. Maybe that's what she meant when, after telling me she was suicidal, she added, "I know you'll be okay. It's your brother I'm worried about."

I didn't know the word *delusion* then, but I could sense its sticky shadows. And I began to beat the darkness back, using my limbs as flares to alert teachers, father, grandparents, aunts, uncles, friends, anyone watching. I was trying to tell them with my erasing, my falling, that something was very, very wrong. As I had with dance, I used my body, but this time it wasn't *jetés* or jazz kicks. It was rage dressed up in party clothes and a popping red lip.

Find the anger.

As a young girl, I'd been well behaved. Demure, if exuberant, always with a "thank you" and a "yes, please." I was obedient and respectful of grown-ups. Naturally diplomatic, or at least, that's what I'd been told. Mom called me an "old soul," and though I didn't know what that meant, exactly, I tried to measure up to its implications. I couldn't help or save or leave my mother. So I did what I could, which was listen. My value became in listening, holding, carrying. She poured her stories into me without regard for my capacity. But I could not get angry at her, not really, not with the violence I needed to erect solid walls, because I also relied on her for food, shelter, love.

So I played the role assigned, urgently swallowing everything that might harm her, including my own rage. The truth is, I quickly learned which conversations and ways of being funneled my family's love and support toward me, and which of my needs threatened to divert the stream.

I learned not to tell my wealthy grandparents that I lived in a one-room motel and shared a king bed with my little brother and mother.

I learned not to tell my father about Mom's confusing stories because his world was measured by twice-daily meditation, his life aligned toward peace, and my life did not reflect those qualities.

I learned not to talk to Mom about sunny afternoons on my grandparents' yacht or trips in progressively smaller planes to their family home in the Bahamas.

I learned that each of my worlds did not have space for the truths of the other. So I ate those truths and poured my sweet being into the provided containers. I learned to stretch and bend my girl body to reflect what they wanted me to be.

No one had silenced me, exactly. It doesn't always happen like that. My quieting was learned and contingent. I get it now: being an old soul meant I was expected to understand things beyond my years. Things I could only perform an understanding of. As the schism between what was true and what was allowed to be true grew too wide, I fell into a blank space.

A girl, dying.

For all the years since her death, fourteen now, my story was that my mother was everything: my home, my spiritual warrior guide, my provider, my feminist model, my confidante, best friend, first love. Those things remain true, but she also groomed me to take more than I should. Taught me how to form my body into a clay jar to hold the spillage of her. I see now this is always happening to girls.

Girls are carrying too much. We are spilling over, top-heavy and destabilized, but praised for our maturity and adaptability if we take it, denigrated if we do not. Trained not to rage, we work in code, our bodies the medium. We eat anger and quietly metabolize it to keep you comfortable.

Find the anger.

I'm angry at my mother for asking too much of me but being unable to ask for help herself.

At my father for not asking at all. At my grandparents for worrying about how a girl should present herself rather than who she should be.

I'd been good, see, but it didn't matter. Because the first time I wasn't, they dropped me. Teachers turned their backs on me. Maybe they'd assumed it was coming. *With a mother like that,* they figured. Another broken girl biting the statistically predetermined dust. My family called it rebellion or divadom or hormones. They called it anything but the anger that I had earned.

I'm angry that the language of spirituality, of maturity, of poise, and of grace all contain directives for ladyhood. That they function as encoded suppression. I'm angry that we've been taught to swallow our pain to save you. That a girl dancing can become a girl drowning and a girl dying so fast.

It wasn't just me. The ones who carried me back to life were a band of wild, raging girls hurting themselves because they couldn't, they wouldn't, hurt you. Cheyenne swallowed a bottle of pills because she was angry. Mandy hitchhiked alone up the I-5 because she was angry. Sam leapt from the balcony and hit the cement because she was angry.

Listen to me.

Teen girls are not divas or drama queens or rebels with no cause. We are here to tell you something and we are using our bodies to wake you the fuck up. We are brave beasts lighting our limbs afire to illuminate darkness. Burning our bodies, like monks did, "as a lamp for help." We are half-born forms, prosaic and didactic, arrogant even. We are not polished to please you. We are divining rods, writhing sensory portals that perceive injustice in our fingernails. Hound dogs for hypocrisy. We are young and naïve and wild and our language may be crude, but if we are angry, you must crack us open. Pick us up like a rock and look underneath, you cowards. We will reveal your secrets and your shame. Like extracting a piece of glass long-embedded in your foot, cutting you cutting you cutting you, we must get it out at all costs.

Only then will we dance again, free and uninhibited.

My Name and My Voice

REEMA ZAMAN

I stand before my husband, holding a heart-shaped cake in my hands, one of the three Valentine's presents I've prepared for him. He lounges on our bed, next to his other gifts, two children's books bought for him to read to our future children and an ice cream maker because ice cream is his favorite food. As he toys with pieces of hastily torn gift-wrapping paper, he regales me with stories of women he flirted with tonight while bartending.

I shiver in my tiny pink-and-white satin-and-lace nightgown from Victoria's Secret, procured and worn because I am a good wife, and I pride myself on doing my duty well. I hug the still-warm cake to my torso to no avail; the chill of his words incites a quick-spreading net of goosebumps over my body. Tiny knots, rioting their resistance, warning my body of danger.

Adding to the chill are the drafts of frigid February air blowing through our home. He and I live in a half-demolished, partially burnt barn deep in upstate New York surrounded by banks of snow. He bought this structure two years ago, with the goal of turning it into a family home. Progress has come in sporadic spits. We lack built-in heating, indoor plumbing, lighting, and cooking capability. In their place, we have a few space heaters, light bulbs strung from the rafters, a hot plate, and, for other needs, the woods behind the barn.

His loyalty to our life together has faded with his momentum in rebuilding the barn. Although initially full of love, charisma, and commitment, he is radically different from the man I fell in love with. Or, perhaps more accurately, he is completely unlike the man I made myself believe he was by focusing on what I longed to see and averting my eyes from forewarning. When we began dating, he explained to me that he was a civil engineer, had started a degree in architecture, and after an apprenticeship with an established firm, he would be able to put his training into practice. Only upon marriage did it become clear he had no intention of following through.

Human beings are vehicles of energy, and all energy must be used either to create or destroy. All bullies hold within them a centrifugal core of insecurity. Feeling small, listless, and willfully purposeless, he has focused his energy on destroying me. In my mouth, I hold hostage my voice, and in this home, he holds me. To voice any feeling would be heresy committed against the universal contract of being a good girl, obedient daughter, loving wife. And so, I don't. I coo and coddle, bend and comply, acquiescing to his needs, moving around his anger like water around stone.

Every morning, every night, I, a feminist for heaven's sake, wake up and fall asleep stunned by the state of my life. I am beginning to trace the story of how we came to be. Every week, every month, I compliantly pour my earnings into this house, the car, our many bills. As he speaks of the other women, it occurs to me that although I devote my every cent to our marital belongings, I have no legal ownership or claim to anything— only his name appears on each contract and lease. Similarly, although only I handle the emotional labor of calming and tending to his needs and moods, only he reaps the benefits, while I am perpetually exhausted and emotionally malnourished. Whenever his temper strikes and he decides to throw a tantrum, he tells me I am his wife for "greensies," not "realsies," to remind me that my green card was procured through marriage. To remind me that I am legally dependent on him, that his love can be withdrawn so easily.

Occasionally, when I was younger and before I knew better, I committed treason by voicing my indecorous anger. At eighteen, I spoke out against a serial predator, a teacher in my high school, only to be quickly silenced by the adults around me. At twenty, I was briefly disowned for speaking too assertively against my father. Having paid the price for voicing my anger, I've inadvertently conspired in creating an abusive marriage built on internalized punishment, with a man who prefers me small and quiet. I've been taught that love is compromise.

Complicit in my slow disappearance, I have managed, though, to hold solid a few things: my own surname and my stubborn attachment to my inner voice, through my daily writing. He mocks the latter, resentful that the quiet, safe space of my mind is the one landscape he cannot enter, let alone damage. Sometimes, when I go on my daily run through the surrounding woods, I recite, "My name and my voice. My name and my voice. My name and my voice." Some days, I whisper my mantra for the full seven, eight, ten miles, as though the sentence were an umbilical cord anchoring me to Mother Earth. So much has been taken, but not these things. I have been running longer and longer lengths to feel that amid his chaos and my erasure I retain the certainty of my limbs, my breath, myself.

Looking at him sprawled on our bed, my mind whispers, *My name and my voice.* I realize now that I don't know the meaning of my first or last name. I should.

"Why are you speaking like this again?" I ask, making sure to keep my tone gentle and compassionate, a dove to his dragon. "I don't mean to complain or antagonize, but when you speak of wanting or going after other women, it hurts my feelings."

We are miles away from any other house or human, so remote from civilization that we lack cell reception. I fear what could happen were I to speak too assertively.

He reaches for his cake, eating with his hands. He laughs, chews, and shrugs. "Baby, you want me to be happy, don't you? I deserve to be happy. Men are men. I can't help it."

In an instant, his words pull me through time, to when I was eleven, in Bangladesh, feeling a cousin, twenty years my senior, approach like incoming rain. I knew to anticipate him partly from instinct, the way the earth knows to expect a storm, and partly because I had been warned by others in my family. He tried, but thankfully, from knowledge inborn and gathered, I escaped. Brimming with fury, I ran to my father to share what had nearly occurred.

"Boys will be boys," he replied, reciting what he had been taught. "It happens, especially between cousins."

I remember seething with such grief I thought I would catch flame.

Decades later, here I stand, the words "men are men" echoing "boys will be boys," searing my heart like a family crest, branding my husband's mark upon my naked, waiting chest.

I breathe into the hollow of my belly, and the inhale travels to reach and touch my resident hunger. Since age fifteen, my anorexia has been ever present. This self-ordered starvation is a habit I've perfected and practiced for as long as I've quieted my words.

I look around, absorbing the details of my surroundings, seeing for the first time the truth of what I have considered "home": coerced captivity, through economic, geographic, and legal dependency, an entrapment built partially by my hands. Compounded by the fact that I have been encouraged to do my all to be small in voice body, mind, and spirit.

The two are inextricably linked: for the normalized existence of male abuse to continue and persist, it requires our shrinking.

My husband licks his fingers. "This cake is great. Want some?"

"No, thank you, honey. I made it for you."

Anorexia, however and whenever it strikes, blooms from a woman's desperate desire for a semblance of control through punishing perfectionism to counteract a world that excels at denying women power, voice, and kindness. Remember, all matter is energy, including emotion, and energy must be used either to create or to destroy. In my teens and twenties, the abusers and years stacked, and with each new wound came abject silence from those around me. As I swallowed my fury for the assaults inflicted and ignored by others, my rage, having nowhere else to go, began its devouring.

With each predator, the cousin at age eleven, the teacher at eighteen, the rapist at twenty-three, the employer at twenty-four, I have burned with unvoiced rage so enormous and bright that from the very onset of my illness, I have been expert at anorexia. Although others may report that denying oneself physical care, rest, and food requires laborious effort, it never has for me. My frothing fury, birthed by multiple heartbreaks, is so mighty that if it orders my body to not eat for a day, a week, my body dutifully complies.

The permission to feel emotion, express thought, and be heard by others is required to feel fully human. I am evidence that when that permission is denied and our voice is silenced, our capacity for being alive begins to diminish, while our capacity for hurting ourselves increases. Blood loses warmth, flesh loses softness, heart loses longing, mind loses clarity. All fluttering urges of hunger, for nourishment, intimacy, belonging, connection, evaporate from the body. Slowly, so does the ability to expect and ask for kindness from others. Through the combination of assaults and the silences that followed, I harbor now a perilous tolerance for abuse.

My husband burps. "I'm full. You're so good to me."

"Thank you, love."

He yawns, loudly. Flecks of cake speckle his stubble. Some fall onto the bed. I busy myself with brushing them aside, take the pan from his hands, and wrap the remains of his feasting. Following my learned rhythm, I pick up and put away his fallen jacket, socks, and shoes. My hand brushes against a crumpled receipt from his bar. On it is scrawled a woman's name and cell number.

Seeing another woman's name sends a bolt of adrenaline through me. Not of jealousy or pain or sorrow, but of solidarity. It dawns on me that by remaining silent, year upon year, I have enabled him to disrespect not only me but her too. To use both her and I as interchangeable morsels.

To speak, then, would be for her and me.

"Sweetheart," I say, as I bend and tidy. "I don't think 'men are men' can be used as justification for your actions. I feel that—"

139

"Oh, come on," he scoffs, raising his volume to override mine. He takes the receipt from my hand, gestures it for emphasis. "You're being dramatic. Don't be oversensitive. It's not a big deal."

For years, I have bitten my tongue, thinking that by maintaining my composure, by rationalizing and forgiving his behavior, by contorting and compromising to the weight of him, I have been but performing correctly, honoring my loyalty to him, my marriage, and my learned identity. I've been taught that men of any kind, be they our abuser, father, or partner, are our mystery to solve, our duty to abide, our pain to nurse, our responsibility to care for, our child-master to defer to.

My husband has taken off his shirt and jeans and has cozied under the covers. Catching me watching, he flashes his gorgeous, all-American, golden-boy grin. The slip of paper with the other woman's name has floated again to the floor. How casually he forgets us.

My name and my voice, implores my mind, reminding me to breathe, reminding me of who I am and to whom I belong. *My name and my voice*.

I've been taught to mistrust my anger because patriarchy has misdiagnosed female anger, thinking its origins to be similar to those of male anger. However, my entire life I have registered rage for very different reasons than the men I've known. I've been raised to be a nurturer, continually cognizant of others, devoted to the collective harmony. When I've felt—when I feel—anger, it is spurred by witnessing and experiencing injustice. In contrast, my husband, like most men, was raised to be an individualistic creature, taught to be driven by personal gain in the form of status, power, and wealth. And women. Thus, he is provoked to anger when his ego and territory have been threatened.

My anger signals the presence of injustice. His tends to flare in the presence of personal insult. Rather than being shameful, my rage is *noble*. Were the world built in honor of the female psyche, wars would be entered and battled according to ethics.

All this to say that now, were I to incite battle, I would be entirely in the right.

A clear, hot line races up my torso and out my mouth. I birth this comet. Call it my voice. My rage. My integrity. My love for myself, the child I was, the children I will have, the other women I am connected to. Whatever its name, it roars:

"NO. This cannot be my life. I was born for a story so much bigger than what you're trying to make of me. I was born for life beyond you."

His pupils dilate, his skin flushes pink. He laughs. Then, seeing that his reaction to me has no effect, he grows furious. He fumes, he yells, he paces. I wash my face, brush my teeth, get into bed. He tries still to pull my attention. I refuse to look his way. For a while I write on my laptop, until slowly, my mind having deposited the day's words into the page before me, satisfaction lulls my eyelids. I shut my laptop, set it down on the floor beside the bed, and sleep.

A few weeks after that fateful Valentine's evening, he evicts me from our home.

In the days following, to affirm my sense of self, I look into the origins of my name. I learn that Reema is another name for Durga, the Indian Warrior Goddess, Protector and Healer of the Wounded World. The fierce incarnation of the divine mother, Durga is defined by her willingness to unleash her anger, to destroy the old in order to create and empower the new.

When drawing up our divorce agreement, I ask for nothing aside from complete detachment from him, which ultimately is everything. My name and my voice are all I need.

Inherited Anger

MARISA SIEGEL

My three-year-old is taking a "Preschool Broadway" class once a week after school. Ten tired, hungry children amble around a classroom as the instructor herds them onto a rug. When most of the children are gathered, she asks them to name feelings. "Sad," "happy," "angry," and "scared" are all called out eagerly. She then asks them to express those feelings on their faces. My son bares his teeth in an exaggerated grin, widens his blue eyes in surprise, turns his mouth down in a frown.

Later, my son tells me he didn't like this exercise. When I ask why, he says, "I don't have an angry face." I promise you, my son *does* have an angry face, but one he evidently cannot fake. Anger is a feeling that we have not talked much about. We've discussed "sad," "scared," and "frustrated." So why not anger? Because I've carefully cultivated a world for him that is free from it.

Anger was pervasive in my childhood home and, eventually, in me. I learned my father was an addict when I was eight.

I began to distance myself from him at sixteen. At twenty-one, I cut all ties.

I've guarded my son from anger because as a child, I never knew a day without it.

I screamed at my father to stop the car.

He swerved the Corolla over to the side of the road, sending empty soda cans, potato chip bags, and assorted debris flying across its floor. My father's car always smelled dank, like a Florida swamp or high school locker room. He stopped just short of jumping the curb, and the half-open passenger door which had been swinging wildly back and forth during the fifty-miles-per-hour, five-block drive from my school slammed shut. I pushed it open again, stumbling into the chilly autumn night, and he sped off.

Tears covered my cheeks, now stinging from the cold. I imagined them freezing onto my face, creating permanent tear-tracks. The moon was bright in the sky, visible even through the storm clouds. The suburban streets of the town I'd lived in my whole life, safe and familiar in daylight, felt menacing in the wet dark. I was about a mile from home; it would have taken my father just a few minutes to drive me to our house before picking my mom up from the LIRR train station, as he was tasked to do. My mom wouldn't have minded waiting; she would have preferred the supposed safety of the car ride to her sixteen-year-old daughter walking a mile alone at night. Her workdays were long and another five minutes wouldn't have mattered much. But my father was high on cocaine and wouldn't listen to reason—he kept insisting I ride with him to the train station, and I knew I couldn't stand to be in the car with him for that long in the state he was in.

I will never ride in the car with my father again, I thought as I made my way home.

For each of the fifteen minutes it took to get to my house, I heard my father's voice yelling *selfish bitch* over and over. Every drop of icy rain made me angrier. As I stepped in a puddle and felt the water soak through my Vans, I prayed something— anything—would happen to him before he got to the train station. My embarrassment and hurt froze into a steely anger. My chest taut, it was as if a belt had been strapped around me and was being pulled tighter and tighter.

Although it would be half a decade before I said the words "my dad was abusive" aloud, I'd known this truth since I was very young. I started compiling a list in my head, as if preparing to make my case in court: the anxiety eight-year-old me felt in preparing to ask my mother if my father was a "drug addict," and what those words meant; the birthday party at my house when he'd been high and terrorized me and my eleven-year-old friends by donning a leftover Halloween zombie mask, scream- ing, and running around the backyard; the numerous times he'd left incest porn open on the family computer; my first day of sixth grade, when he'd called out "who's that hottie?" as I walked into my new school . . . it was a list without end.

This high-speed, coked-up ride halfway home from school had to be the last straw. How could my mother hear about what happened this evening, alongside all that had happened before, and permit my father to continue living in our house? He'd put me in immediate physical danger, driving at fifty miles per hour down those sleepy, twenty-five-miles-per-hour suburban streets. He'd shown up at school wired on cocaine, again. Perhaps she'd throw him out that very night.

I reached my front yard, paused, and took a deep breath. The Corolla was not back in the driveway yet. I had a few more minutes before my parents returned to gather my wits and to figure out how to insist to my mother that living with my father wasn't safe for me. I ran up the stairs to my bedroom, threw my bag onto the floor, and sank into my bed.

When my mother appeared at my door, I launched into an account of what had happened that night. I ran through my culled list of examples of his worst behavior from years past. I sat on my bed, one hand gripping its painted-white metal frame, the other gesturing frantically in the air. "I can't live in the same house as him anymore!"

"What do you want me to say, Marisa?" She sounded exhausted, defeated. "Do you want to go and live with your grandparents?" She began to quietly cry.

That night, my mother couldn't save me.

I didn't respond to her question. Instead, I yelled for her to leave me alone, slamming the bedroom door for emphasis. I sat on the bed in stunned silence. Did I want to go live with my grandparents? How incredibly fucking unfair. My grandparents lived forty minutes away from my school and my friends, in an apartment in Queens across the street from a senior citizens' recreational facility. I wasn't the problem. Why should I be the one to be forced out?

I unclenched my fingers from the bedframe and wiped my face. My anger filled my bedroom.

At sixteen, I understood that my mother was never going to kick my father out of the house. However wrong that was, and however right I was that living with him was cruel and unsafe, didn't matter. It was going to be my job to protect myself.

I grabbed a pen and a notebook out of my backpack, and began to write.

I still recall exactly the letter I hastily scrawled to my father that night. Addressing him by his first name, I wrote that he was no longer a parental authority in my life. If he insisted on speaking to me, I would just pretend I couldn't hear. The letter ended with a threat: If he wanted any hope of meeting the children I might one day have, he would stay out of my way.

Of course, he didn't. But from that day forward, I built a wall. Each time he'd throw an insult in my direction, crack a dirty joke, or come home with those red-tinged eyes, that wall was reinforced. I stopped hearing him. It was no small feat to pretend that a two-hundred-pound coked-up gorilla-man didn't live in the same house as me, but my anger was louder than my father could ever be.

My anger culminated when I was twenty-one, when my dad—dead to the world following another cocaine binge—was supposed to let me into the house to pick up my laundry. I was no longer living at home, but my mom assured me he'd be there and would leave the door unlocked.

I knocked till my knuckles ached. I screamed like a maniac on our front porch. I cried fiery hot tears. The bag of laundry I couldn't get to became every day my dad had ruined, every terrifying moment he'd put me through. I wanted that bag of laundry, and I was going to get it.

And so, I punched through a window.

Shards of glass flew around me like diamonds. If it hurt, I don't remember the pain. If it made a sound, I didn't hear it. Neither did my father, who, unconscious somewhere upstairs, did not wake up, even after I climbed inside and stood shaking and shrieking in our dining room.

There was something beautiful about the glass exploding into diamonds. I think, maybe, the beautiful thing was me, allowing my anger to manifest.

Our family cat stared at me and the piles of shattered glass at my feet. It was the cat's stare that broke my anger. I had never been—and am still not—the kind of person who lashes out. I very rarely "lose it." But after that day, there was no denying my anger's power. As a woman, as a writer, and now as a mother, I have been punching through windows ever since.

While pregnant, I worried about genetics. When interviewing pediatricians who inevitably asked for family health history, I had to acknowledge my father's existence in my DNA, the DNA I shared with my unborn son. I wondered at what age my son would ask about my father—and at what age I'd be able to answer honestly.

Mostly, I was terrified that my son might resemble my father. That he'd inherit the "bad genes." That I might raise a bad man, a selfish man, the kind of man who could hurt a child. That I'd raise an addict. How could I prevent this unborn person from becoming a man like the man who'd raised me?

But our genes don't define us. Blood doesn't make family. I've had to push against science and social norms, push against relatives and friends who feel differently, to insist upon these truths for myself. From age sixteen on, I refused to concede that my father's blood relation to me had to mean anything at all. I went through the lengthy, frustrating process of legally changing my once-hyphenated last name to my mother's maiden name. I spoke plainly about my situation at home to teachers, therapists, and family members but only mentioned my father when asked directly about him and usually to explain that he was not to be treated as a parental authority.

Friends from college assumed my father was dead, or absent, not living twenty feet from my childhood bedroom and still married to the mother I mentioned frequently and with affection. I was all the proof I needed to believe that it was possible to redefine what "family" meant in everyday life.

But realizing I was going to become a mother, feeling the weight of what lay ahead, meant acknowledging that my father was a part of me so that I could best ready myself to be a better parent than my parents had been to me.

My father died the week my son was born. A small gift, but I cannot dig his DNA out of my son and me, where it hides in our warm and alive bodies. But instead of feeling powerless, I remember that the same blood flowing through my veins today flowed through me when I survived that history.

I've written through my anger for most of my life, but I'd never interrogated it until I began to parent my son. I'd never thoughtfully asked questions of it.

Anger, why do you stay? Anger, what do you give me? Anger, what do you cost me?

As a mother, I've turned these questions over in my mind often. I am thankful to my anger for protecting me, as a child and into adulthood. My anger has fueled me, has given me energy and a will to succeed even when I am floundering. When I am afraid, I feel that fear as anger—and I know I can face it down. I know I can control it.

The intensity of my anger is matched by the intensity of my love. I don't truly want or expect for my child to never experience anger. Rather, I want his early years to be focused on feeling secure, so that when he does get angry, he is able to trust that he can feel those feelings and share them with his family if he wants to. He'll know that I will help him when he is feeling angry, that I will work to understand his anger. He will feel supported in those ways in which I was not; he will not be a child navigating adult circumstances alone. He will not have the childhood I had, because I know how to do better.

My son looks only like me, like his father, and like himself. I do not see my father in him. He is not growing up steeped in rage. His childhood is not a war against blood. He understands family as the people who love you and who you choose to love, and he understands home as safety and comfort.

My son will inherit many behaviors and ailments and anxieties from me, but he will not inherit my lifetime of anger. Instead, he will benefit from the ways I've learned to turn anger into action. He will learn that anger can be motivating rather than limiting, and that we can manage how our anger expresses itself. He will punch through his own windows, and I will be cheering him on when he does.

I will determine carefully which pieces of my childhood to share with him, and when, but I will share—and that sharing will become one of the ways I teach my son to be a good man, a man who is nothing like my father.

On the Back Burner

DANI BOSS

I am a walking middle finger. My heart thrums to the bassline of my newly discovered anthem: "Killing in the Name Of" by Rage Against the Machine. The band likely didn't write it for middle-aged, perimenopausal women. The song is about so much more, but for me the meaning is personally distilled as the lead singer first speaks, then screams the thing I'd like to say most: "Fuck you / I won't do what you tell me!"

I've begun really cranking this one when I'm alone in the car, shaking my head like a pissed-off lead singer while I holler through the sunroof. All of this only takes place on the open road. At stoplights, I turn it down and behave. I was raised to be a good girl. I may scream that I won't do what you tell me, but the likelihood is that I will.

My first whiff of *The Change* came at bedtime, but not in hot flashes. I was trying to explain my frustration to my husband, Trevor. We have a blended family, with four parents for two kids. Most of the time that means we have other adults to rely on when things get hairy. To me, that should mean that we are more efficient than a traditional family because there's almost always backup. But my stepson's football helmet had been forgotten in the midweek household shuffle, and his first practice was the following day. The blood rattled around in my veins. My heart pounded songs of war.

Trevor wondered why it was a big deal, why I couldn't just let it go. "Will this be important in a year? It's just a forgotten helmet," he offered.

"Just? *Just?* Do you have any idea what this is going to do to my day tomorrow? The coach has to be called. An alternate time to pick it up has to be arranged. Now I'm going to inconvenience other people because we can't handle ourselves. It's possible that he will miss practice tomorrow because the adults couldn't manage a simple task. We look lazy, incompetent, and uninterested in our kid's life. This is *not* nothing."

Trevor sighed. "Have you read *The Miracle of Mindfulness* yet?" he asked. "I really think it could help."

I rolled my eyes. He had been trying to get me to read this book for months. He thought it would help my increased moodiness if I learned to live in the moment. It probably would, but I didn't want to stifle my anger anymore. I wanted to rage.

Searing tears began to fall, which just made me angrier. I paced the room, gesturing in a way that suggested I was trying to subdue a large, wild bird, and persisted in trying to make Trevor as mad as I was, with no luck.

"A book can't fix this. Things used to annoy me, but now I hate them and want them dead." My anger, so long repressed, had risen closer to the surface of my skin.

I clicked off the light and pressed my teeth against my lower lip to form the *F* that began my silent protest to the darkness. *Fuck you!* My core tightened. My throat closed shutter-fast around the hard *-ck*. Keeping the *you* silent was easier. This was not how I spoke to people. I didn't recognize myself this angry.

A trip to the gynecologist followed. My symptoms? Being forty-nine, telling the kids working at a fast-food joint that they needed a grown-up on shift, chasing down an irresponsible driver to tell him that cutting me off was "a dick move," howl-crying in the closet when I felt there was nothing to wear. There was no blood test that would confirm it, but she'd seen enough women in tears, shocked at their own rage to confirm: perimenopause had arrived. The doctor couldn't prescribe anything for relief right away unless I wanted to start hormones. I didn't, so I'd just have to slog through it and come back if I wasn't feeling better.

And slog I have. What am I supposed to do with this anger, so long tamped-down and unexpressed? I have no elegant plan for transitioning into a take-no-shit approach. A lifetime of saying yes to things I didn't want to do—unpaid after-school meetings at my teaching job, extending myself in relationships with no regard for my own comfort—left me feeling like a mug-shot-in-waiting. Any minute now, I'd lose it, and only women my age would nod with understanding as I was carted off to jail. But I have no role model to measure my outbursts by. Healthy examples of boundaries and how to express one's anger were absent in my youth.

I never saw a woman I knew speak her mind in the moment she felt wronged. The few women I did know who defended their psychological space were thought of as unhinged or un-disciplined, as much by women as by men. They were called names like "bitch" and "hysterical." I learned from the women I respected that anger was not our place.

The only safe place I saw for women to release their anger was among other, trusted women. My mom and her best girl-friends planned venting parties when the men were away. Their grievances were a surprise to me, not because I hadn't witnessed things they should be pissed about, but because they hadn't shown much sign of distress in the moment. Equally surprising was the abundance of seventy-five-percent-off-post-Halloween candy. Women hauled it out of cavernous purses and slapped it down on the coffee table. An offering? The price of admission? They filled their guts even as they spilled them. Sometimes they smoked, leaving a barfly haze that somehow cushioned the things they talked about. We girls were sent to play while they talked, but we heard pieces of the conversation, usually about men: ". . . yells at the kids all the time," ". . . flirting with Suzie the Floozy!" ". . . tailgates like a crazy person." The amber-toned, seventies living room of Mom's best friend was the place for all the words to come out that they had been waiting to say.

Phrases like, "I wish I would have said . . ." often preceded sentiments of deep frustration. Sometimes a woman in the room would say she had said something shockingly honest or confrontational—"So I was, like, 'Don't you talk to me like that! You're the one with the problem!'" When asked if she had really said that, she would admit quickly that, no, she hadn't. But she sure wished she had. Nobody blamed her. They all understood that the clarity and the words would sometimes come after the moment of anger.

In this way, I began to believe that anger was not the province of women. All these secret-squirrel meetings during which so much female anger was unleashed contrasted sharply with their silence about these issues everywhere else. A tight-lipped, squinty smile is what I learned could repress anger.

Rage was the dominion of men, who seemed to have unlimited social safety. My mother showed me how to respond to an angry man: lowered head, those tight lips, and attending to every detail that might end this particular tantrum or ward off the next. Be meek. Get small. Stay busy. Men emitted. Women absorbed.

The child of a very angry father, I learned young that my best shot at getting praise was to run myself ragged trying to please him. I happily dangled in his arms upside-down in car engines to turn wrenches in spaces too small for his big hands. I brought him cold drinks and bowls of salty snacks he hadn't asked for. I learned that my role as a girl was to try to keep the peace through my work and my silence. I decided his moods were my responsibility; the only possibility for his approval and family happiness was through my service.

My father's anger could stop traffic. The road we grew up on had a twenty-five-mile-per-hour speed limit, but people treated it more like a freeway. If Dad saw someone coming down our road too fast, he greeted them in the street, puffing himself up like a wild animal, screwing up his face into something menacing. He would point right at the driver's face as if issuing some kind of ancient Sicilian curse, and bellow, "SLOW DOWN!" with all his might. His voice echoed deep in his barrel chest and didn't lose power as it dispersed into the atmosphere. My father's yelling unperched birds.

He took on the Coast Guard, Canadian border agents, and the cashiers at RadioShack. Nobody ever questioned his right to rage. He did not seem to suffer consequences socially. Because of him, I knew that angry men were powerful and dangerous. It was best to avert your eyes and become as invisible as possible when they began to yell, as if by being still one could avoid becoming a target. This is also how I imagine one would act in the presence of a velociraptor.

Now that my estrogen is receding, I have fury that rivals my father's. And though his had all the free air to expand into, mine is constantly made unwelcome. Yelling is avoided in my marriage. It's an agreement I made, and one I want to live by. But lately, it's harder. When I break the rule, I'm reminded that yelling doesn't feel good to the listener. I'm cautioned: don't be like your father. Girlfriends interrupt a rant with a hand on my forearm. "Dani," they say, as if trying to bring me back to myself. The worst is when someone obviously tries to change the subject just when I'm getting started. I comply. I comply, but only because the part of me that wants to be liked is a little stronger than my fury.

I hated Dad's rage, how he seemed so incapable of controlling it, how it made me so scared and small. I resented him for taking it out on us all the time, and the way it changed what I thought of my own value. I do not want to taint my stepchildren's experience with me by letting my anger affect who they become. Bellowing, howling anger has been written on top of my DNA. It's how I want to respond to frustration. But because I was also taught to be a good girl and keep it to myself, my anger feels warped into something even more unnatural than hateful. I resent that, too.

I recently heard my stepdaughter grumble as she came to the pantry to help me clean late one night when we'd been working to ready the house for entertaining.

"Gosh, boys, feel free to help," she whispered. I recognized her frustration in no time. The boys were sitting on the couch, done for the day. I was still working. She felt a gendered kinship and responsibility that they did not. The inequity ticked her off, but she could only air that to me. I stopped cleaning and suggested she speak to them about it. She couldn't. I understood and didn't force her. But then we were both mad. As sure as she is becoming a woman, she is also being indoctrinated into a system I recognize—one that rewards female martyrdom with adoration and gratitude but leaves little room for her to air her frustration. I told her it was okay to be angry and to say so. That her anger doesn't have to hide in the pantry.

That night I sent my stepdaughter back out to the couch to relax with her father and brother. I hope she'll learn to regulate her anger by both examining and expressing it. I hope I can help her. I'm still trying to figure out how to help myself. At midlife, I have withstood enough baloney. My anger feels righteous and I feel entitled, after so much silence, to let it rain on all of creation. But that's not how I was raised. It might look more like a drizzle. It might look like a copy of *The Miracle of Mindfulness* sailing across my living room.

"Basic Math"

MEREDITH TALUSAN

I must have made a mistake, I thought in the face of my class-mate Nathaniel's ire. It was 2006, and I was a student in Cornell's fiction MFA program, four years post–gender transition and undisclosed to colleagues in my new environment. He was giving a craft lecture for the fifteen other students, one of our class requirements in which we were supposed to discuss a nuts-and-bolts aspect of fiction.

He'd handed out a set of graphs meant to illustrate various relationships between story structure and time. One of the graphs was inaccurate; it was supposed to illustrate flashbacks but was drawn with lines that implied time was moving backward, like a video on rewind. This isn't how flashbacks work— you can jump back to another time, but actions move forward once you get there.

I raised my hand.

"Would it be possible for you to clarify the second graph?" I asked. I proceeded to conjecture that it might not accurately represent what he was explaining, and maybe there was a way to present it differently. I had spent two years as a technical assistant at MIT routinely designing figures like these and had pored through books and articles on how to present similar information effectively, so I knew how to make the graph more accurate. But I soft-pedaled my feedback for fear he would take it the wrong way. I'd learned since I began to present myself as a woman that it's better to frame my criticism of men in the form of a question rather than as a statement, or worse, an assertion, so the man can correct himself with no damage to his self-esteem.

Despite going out of my way to be deferent, Nathaniel took my question badly. He seemed affronted by even the implication of my challenge, so he re-drew the exact same graph on the board and repeated the exact same explanation he'd gone through five minutes before with the same inaccuracies, still diagramming exactly the opposite of what he was saying, making time move backward rather than jumping from point to point. And when he finished, he asked me whether I now understood.

"I'm still confused," I said, and hoped he would finally correct himself. Maybe I should have told him point-blank how the graph could be made accurate, but it seemed too late for that, since my first question had already rankled him.

"This is basic math, Meredith," he replied. That was when I thought for a moment that I must be wrong, before another part of me realized I was letting Nathaniel undermine my judgment just because he was a man. Even though he had so much less experience designing graphs than I did, all the unconscious messages I had absorbed about women being less capable at math had permeated my brain, and him invoking "basic math" activated my self-doubt. I sat in shock at myself while Nathaniel continued his lecture.

Had this happened prior to transition, I would have simply pointed out his error, and if he questioned me, I would have insisted I was right and demonstrated why. We probably wouldn't have had the confrontation to begin with, since he would have just bowed to a man with more expertise. But as a woman, my mind threw out all those experiences, at least unconsciously, at least in that classroom.

I didn't become a woman to simply absorb all of society's assumptions about gender. I don't think gender is something you can swap like a coat, one day deciding you're a woman and therefore taking on all the trappings of womanhood and leaving behind the trappings of manhood. It's more like an equalizer, with numerous channels that control aspects of how the world sees you; mine was once tuned toward a male default standard, and then shifted to female through transition. But I don't believe you ever quite lose what you left behind. You take on your new role in a way that's different from those who have been seen as girls and women their whole lives. Having been raised a boy meant that my mind consistently saw and refused to accept the many ways that women are made less because of our gender.

But even while my conscious brain saw gender inequality for what it was, my unconscious brain absorbed the notion that I was automatically less capable than a man, even if this defied logic.

Had this incident happened today, after fifteen years of womanhood, I would have navigated it the only way my gender could: I would have used every ounce of self-control to stay calm so I wouldn't be seen as confrontational, yet I would have laced that calmness with just enough assertion that Nathaniel and my classmates would take my judgment seriously. If I was too nice, my ideas would be easily dismissed; too assertive, and I would be branded a bitch.

Because I was new to womanhood, I didn't know I was supposed to let Nathaniel's blatant insult to my intelligence go. Or, if I couldn't let it go, I didn't know that I was supposed to complain about it with women friends behind closed doors so as not to ruffle feathers, to get sympathetic hugs to ease my distress while allowing men to continue treating women the way they wanted. I didn't know that part of being a woman was accepting that it's a man's right to preserve his ego by publicly insulting a woman's intelligence even when he's objectively wrong. And that a woman who takes umbrage over such an act would be unreasonable, nitpicky, even hysterical.

Yet what I didn't know consciously I still manifested outwardly as I stayed quiet through the rest of Nathaniel's lecture, only turning to a friend for confirmation that he was wrong after the class was done. Nathaniel left without talking to me, even when he could see that I was visibly upset, and did not make any gesture of apology over the following days. As I mulled over the incident, I found myself unable to keep quiet about it and fumed over the fact that, as a gesture of care, I babysat Nathaniel's children for free once a week so he and his wife could go out, another one of those kind things I'd observed good women do with no expectation of anything in return. Nathaniel and I instantly ceased communication; I'm sure it hardly surprised him when I didn't show up to babysit his kids and when I told colleagues in our small program that we were no longer friends.

This incident also opened a dam in me, and I decided that I could no longer tolerate the many other instances of sexist behavior I observed in my classes. I pointed out to our fiction workshop professor that he allowed Nathaniel to talk significantly more than he did other people in our workshop group of two men and six women. I also pointed out to that workshop leader and other faculty how Nathaniel gave feedback like he was a professor and not a fellow student, often explaining other students' work from a position of authority rather than as a colleague. I refused to let him and other men interrupt me when I spoke, something that the other women in my program routinely allowed. I became the raging feminist, the one who was quick to point out every instance of gender inequality I observed. But in a social environment that had little interest in creating a microculture where men and women were actually treated equally, this was seen as a great disturbance, and people began to dissociate with me for fear that professors would no longer favor them if they observed that I was their friend.

Near the end of the school year, I had coffee with one of the women who had distanced herself from me, to clear the air and talk about what happened. She was one of the few other women of color in my program, and it disappointed me that she not only withdrew from me but also actively took Nathaniel's side and maintained a close friendship with him. We sat outside on a bench during a warm day in May, after the harshness of Ithaca's winter.

"I just don't understand why you made it such a big deal," she said. "I don't understand why you told other people you didn't want to be his friend."

It was then I realized that I was being punished not just because I overvalued my intelligence as a woman, but because I valued that intelligence over wanting everyone to get along, which is what women are supposed to value above all else. Doing otherwise made me unwomanly. To get along in the world as an intelligent woman, I had to carefully balance these two often-conflicting values, being seen as an intellectual equal while not compromising the harmony of whichever group I belonged to. This was going to take a lot of work, and it's work that I've done and have continued to do ever since—because the way society treats women gives me little choice.

But it was too late for me at Cornell. I was still an MFA student, but I'd alienated the chair of my program—who took great pride in building a model environment and bristled at any challenges to it—so that I wasn't invited to the big party she threw before school started every year, a clear gesture of displeasure that didn't go unnoticed. Writers in MFA programs rely on the support of professors for connections and recommendations, so her lack of support, along with that of other professors in my department, severely compromised my chances of being introduced to the right people, being guided toward the right fellowships—everything I needed to continue my career as a writer.

The writing career I've built has been entirely independent of that MFA program and its professors. After many years of feeling like I had sabotaged myself because I was unable to swallow the sexist norms I encountered there, I was able to find like-minded people through the internet, who confirmed that they had had similar experiences, some of them editors who gave me opportunities to demonstrate my abilities.

I continue to look back at that moment, when I thought myself to be less intelligent than I was in response to a man's challenge, and I realize now that it wasn't just me absorbing social conditioning I could only describe as negative. It was actually my mind trying to protect me from the risks of believing myself to be fully equal to men, despite being a woman. It was my mind trying to force itself to believe I was less, because it would be to my own immediate benefit to believe that, even if doing so collectively kept women down.

If I had learned to make myself small, then I could have had a chance to get along in the world, to hope that a mentor would someday discover my abilities and usher me into success at which I as a woman would marvel in wonder, conditioned to see my talent as a pleasant surprise rather than a quality I knowingly possessed. Making myself small as a woman would have been to my benefit, but I'm glad that I overcame the unconscious temptation to lessen myself, because maybe having fought and continuing to fight—often against my own best interests—would mean that fewer women will need to make themselves less in the future.

The Color of Being Muslim

SHAHEEN PASHA

I've seen my rage as a color since I was a little girl. It started as a game to describe those emotions I didn't yet have words to express. When I was a tomboy with a bowl cut, my rage would float in front of me in shades of blue and dark green, like the ocean I saw at Coney Island. As I became an angsty teen, with large breasts shrouded behind extra-large sweatshirts and my mother's frequent admonitions to hide my rapidly developing figure ringing in my ears, my rage took on the hues of the night sky; purples shimmering beneath the surface of my respectful demeanor.

Pakistani-American Muslim girls in my world did not openly rage against their parents, their older siblings, their teachers, handsy store clerks, or the procession of meddling aunties who ruled our lives. To openly express our anger was to be too American, it was to be disrespectful. So I let the colors dance—a veritable prism in my mind's eye—and marveled at the many shades that emerged every time I swallowed an angry retort or disappeared into my room to avoid a conflict.

But it wasn't until I met Baseemah that my rage took on the steady shade of red. Not just any red; a deep blood maroon that developed over time and screamed of pain and disillusionment, stifled sexuality, and a sense of otherness that ran through my veins. To me, it was the color of being a Muslim American.

I first met Baseemah as a fifteen-year-old high school sophomore in Brooklyn. I walked into Spanish class and there she stood. She had ebony skin, perfect teeth, fitted jeans that gave just a hint of seductive curves, and a red headscarf wrapped around her head like she was a queen. It was the color of Pakistani brides and rubies. It was the color of defiance. And it suited Baseemah. She was confident, radiant, unabashedly Muslim. She was beautiful.

Until that day, I had never seen the beauty in hijab or in being Muslim. In my youth, my Muslim identity was less about religion and more about a cultural expectation within my Pakistani community: pray, learn to read the Arabic letters in the Quran even if you don't understand the meaning, fast during Ramadan. Rinse and repeat. As I became a teenager, additional rules came into the mix: don't wear clothes that highlight your figure, don't go to prom, and don't even think about dating. I couldn't really tell whether the restrictions were based in Islam or my parents' own deep-seated fears that we would somehow lose all ties to our Pakistani roots.

So, I prayed five times a day and put my faith in a God I didn't really question. I didn't see what was so special about being Muslim. To me, it was another aspect of my life that made me different and weird, like my Pakistani identity. They were interchangeable. But hijab was never part of that mix growing up. Not for me and certainly not for most of the other girls in my community, who paraded around Pakistani parties and festivals in colorful Salwar Kameez suits with our hair flowing in the wind, hoping to catch the eyes of the boys while avoiding the gossipy glares of the hovering aunties.

With the exception of a few conservative girls I knew in our circle who had started covering their hair, hijab was what women did in foreign lands filled with camels and dust. Head coverings, beyond the flimsy, sequined chiffon scarves we wore with our Pakistani outfits, belonged to backward villages or were props in the insipid Bollywood movies I watched as a kid. They were certainly not beautiful.

But on Baseemah, an African American Muslim girl with a sense of fashion that would rival any top model's, I saw hijab as a statement, an anthem of Muslim identity. It was a color and a song and I wanted to envelop myself in both.

Baseemah and I became friends and I began to seriously consider wearing hijab. Each day, I would try on a scarf in the bathroom before leaving for school. And each day, I would chicken out, stuffing the material back into my drawer.

The same year I mulled over my secret desire, a van filled with explosives detonated under the North Tower of the World Trade Center. Six people died and a thousand more were injured.

I learned about it that evening when I flipped on the television and was met with static on the screen. My father was worried. He smoked cigarette after cigarette and listened to the radio in silence. I didn't understand why until after the first arrests were made, confirming that the attackers were Muslim. I was running to class when the blond junior varsity track runner I had secretly crushed on for a year bumped into me in the hall. "Oh, I better say sorry to you or you'll throw a bomb or something into the school," he said, backing away, his hands held up defensively. "You all are fucking nuts."

I watched him back off laughing, my smile fading fast. I turned into my social studies class, searching for Baseemah. I couldn't find her. It wasn't until I heard her soft voice in my ear that I realized she was sitting behind me, her hair pulled back into a ponytail, her scarf nowhere to be seen.

"My dad said it wasn't a good idea to be so visible as a Muslim right now," she said. "It makes more sense to look like you, you know, not religious or anything."

In that instant, her red—the jeweled color I had seen Baseemah wear the first day we met—became the darker shade of my muted, internalized rage. I seethed inside, wondering what it would feel like to smack the white boy who insulted me and leave a red handprint across his fair skin. Would it fade away slowly or turn into a bruise, rimmed in blue and purple? I knew I would never find out, but I found solace in the fantasy.

My relationship with Baseemah also changed that day. In her exposed hair, I felt a subtle accusation of cowardice and privilege for my ability to blend among those who hated us, without having to give anything up. We never talked about it, but we drifted apart. I mourned the loss of our friendship and silently raged against the circumstances that tore us apart.

It was a voiceless rage I carried for years. At first, it took aim only at the Islamophobes who made me feel less American despite my blue passport and New York birth. That was an easy rage, unambiguous and pure, directed solely at people who demeaned my faith and identity. They chose to hate me without knowing me. So I detested them back. But, even in that hatred, I found myself trying to maintain a delicate balance that was exhausting.

Anger as a Muslim American is a precarious emotion, layered and complex. Too much anger and you're seen as unstable, a threat to society with jihad coursing through your veins. You're the terrorist-in-hiding, just waiting for the right spark. Too little anger, and you're seen as a passive player, unwilling to condemn the atrocities of a handful of people who have somehow become the mascots of your religion, and therefore complicit in their crimes. And whether I showed my anger or not, I was still representative of that inexplicable Islamic world, governed by strict rules and seemingly odd restrictions on the pleasures of beer and bacon. I was guilty by my association with an Islamic diaspora that somehow kept breeding terrorists who filled endless news cycles with their cries of *Allahu Akbar*.

But I've got a secret to share. I never really belonged to that world either. It's not that I didn't want to belong. But after I moved on to college, away from the strict rules of my parents, I wanted to explore outside of the sheltered world my family and community had created. I didn't want to hide it, like so many others did in my community, living double lives that their parents knew nothing about. My inability to lie made me vulnerable and different. An outsider within my own Muslim community.

So, I reinvented myself. Prayers that had once anchored me suddenly seemed out of place in my life, providing little comfort as I began to search for who I was outside of my religious and cultural identities. But it was my sudden awareness of my body and my desires that truly plagued me. I had grown up with a firm understanding that such pleasures were off limits until marriage. But as I explored my autonomy as a woman, I questioned why my sexuality was haram. I was conflicted. As much as I wanted to feel a man's hands encircle my waist at a New York club, I couldn't enjoy the sensation when it happened. Inevitably I would pull away, caught up in initial feelings of guilt and shame. And then those emotions would darken to anger. Anger at him for violating my space and anger at myself for being unable to feel pleasure in his touch, as my mother's voice rang in my ears, telling me that Muslim girls didn't behave this way. My self-inflicted anger was bright, almost orange, like a flame.

As penance, I would then go to parties within my own Pakistani Muslim community, determined to fit in, to break free of my sinful desires and find comfort in a circle that clearly knew right from wrong. But I didn't belong. My laugh was too loud, my scarf didn't properly cover my blouse, which was too short over my skirt, I caught the attention of too many boys—childhood friends—whose mothers were quick to warn them away. I felt adrift among those I had known my whole life. In their black-and-white world, I was a sorrowful shade of dishwater gray. And I began to realize that many of them pitied me for somehow being less of a Muslim. I was the girl no one would want to marry because I wasn't enough of anything. Not Pakistani enough. Not Muslim enough. Not American enough. Not good enough.

It was a period of free fall. I was untethered and lost. I didn't belong anywhere and the injustice of that filled me with a blinding rage not just at Islamophobes anymore, but at everyone, including my own community.

But acknowledging any rage against my Muslim American community was still, as always, convoluted and tricky. I stewed over their disparaging views of me and my life choices but vehemently defended them to others out of a fierce sense of loyalty. I may have hated some of my community members for their disapproval and their pity, but I was taught never to badmouth our own kind. Criticizing other Muslim Americans would open the door for outsiders to start lobbing insults. It was an invitation for Islamophobes to peg me as an oppressed Muslim woman to be rescued, never understanding that the oppression I felt came from both sides, suffocating and silencing. So I swallowed that anger until it took on another hue for me, a dull, burnt shade of red ochre. It was tinged with abandonment and confusion. It was the shade of judgment.

I fell in love with my best friend. He was a Pakistani Muslim, just like me, but one who embraced both worlds unapologetically. He went to Friday prayers and fasted during Ramadan; he slept with white women and drank alcohol. And he didn't hide it. In my sheltered world of right and wrong, halal and haram, Muslim and non-Muslim, he was a conundrum that somehow made perfect sense to me. For the first time, I let go of my inhibitions, and with his arms around me, I felt a new sense of acceptance and freedom.

In the judgmental, restrictive world we grew up in, the acceptance of mind and body we gave each other was a gift few could offer. Even when it came to my still-conservative views on sex, there was no pressure. He understood and respected my inhibitions and we explored our sexuality together in other ways, an awakening that changed me. I felt I had found a home after years of not belonging anywhere.

And then came the day we stood in my living room, voices raised, our faces mere inches from each other. "You want me to marry you and if it was just about you and me, I know we could be happy," he said. "But it's not. I can't bring you home to my family. You're not the kind of girl that my mother would accept. You just wouldn't fit into my community."

And with those words, the murderous shade of maroon that always lurked beneath the surface, dormant around him, took over. In my rage, I saw the color of the blood I imagined flowing from his light brown eyes, once I scratched them out. It was the same shade my face turned as I used all my willpower to walk away from him.

It was that relationship that broke me. It wasn't the fact that, as a man, he didn't deem me good enough to marry. It was that he seemed to confirm what I had known all along: my inability to conform to either society left me as a pariah in both.

A few days after our relationship ended, I pulled out my prayer mat. I kneeled on it and began to cry. I cried until I had no more tears left, after I was done, I felt a lightness that I had been missing for years. I had spent years swallowing rage over the suffocating expectations of others. First at the outsiders who made me hate myself for being Muslim, then at my own community who made me feel like a stranger for questioning their rigid rules of decorum. And finally, at the man who made me feel accepted only to betray me when I needed more from him. The rage I had been taught as a child to subdue had been eating me alive. But that day, as I rose from my prayer mat, I decided to give it a voice. Unapologetic and loud.

The next day and every day after, I went to work in my fashionably short dresses and skirts and came home to wrap myself in a long scarf and made my evening prayers in the solitude of my bedroom, away from the eyes of anyone else. My prayers became for me alone, a meditation to connect me spiritually with God, rather than a performance by which other Muslims could judge my piety.

Among my non-Muslim friends and coworkers, I started speaking out as a Muslim woman. Comments that I had let slide in the past I now held up for discussion and debate. I wore my religious identity on my sleeve and defied anyone to try to find a disconnect between any aspects of my lifestyle and my beliefs. I no longer hid my anger behind any masks. Instead, I gave my rage free rein in the writings I shared with the world and the public appearances I made as a Muslim woman speaking about my identity. I was no longer afraid to call out the critics in all aspects of my life and hold a mirror to their judgments and fallacies. Months after I made the internal shift to unapologetically be myself, I met a Pakistani Canadian man who fell in love with the very qualities about me that I had long struggled with. We married after a whirlwind courtship and eventually had three children, with strong personalities of their own.

It hasn't been so easy to be vocal as a Muslim American woman over the past few years, though. The 2016 election brought a wave of Islamophobia and xenophobia that shook me to the core, and I often felt it would be easier to simply stay quiet. Baseemah was right all those years ago. I don't look religious in the traditional sense and that gives me a layer of protection. Unlike the many wonderful hijabi women who became my close friends over the years, I have the ability to blend and hide when things get tough. I could always swallow my anger and wait for a better time.

But as the mother of a teenage daughter, I realized very quickly that staying quiet was not an option. She's never been taught to stifle her anger the way I was as a child, for fear of being a pariah in any community. She never needed colors to express her rage because she was given a voice with which to shout it to the world. She is proudly Muslim and American in a world that is increasingly becoming hostile to one half of that identity.

So, I take my cue from my daughter and choose not to hide. Instead, I channel my rage to speak out publicly against both the Islamophobes, who see me as a threat, and the judgmental members of my own community, who seek to shame those they cannot control. I put up with the nasty emails and social media threats from trolls on both sides as well as the thinly veiled criticism I still hear from the conservative members of my extended family. Those experiences made me the color of Muslim I am today, the deep red of my righteous anger.

But I think it may be different for my daughter. Recently, I asked her whether she had ever associated a color with being Muslim. "Pink," she said, with a smile. "The color of love."

Homegrown Anger

LISA FACTORA-BORCHERS

Highway 62 runs through a small town called Alliance. It's a skinny paved road that leads to my brother's house. Along 62, there's no shortage of MAGA signs, Confederate flags drooping from porches, intimidatingly large pickup trucks, and that popular bumper sticker with a graphic of six different guns lined up in a row and the words: "You have your family, I have mine."

Most people don't have a residential home for anger. I do. It's called Ohio. Ohio was always the place where I could see anger clearly, where contention was as clear as the farmlands, expanding deep into the horizon of water towers and beyond. In Ohio, there is space to be angry.

As the daughter of immigrants who grew up listening to stories about the Philippine diaspora, I knew about migration. When I was eight years old, my family moved from New Jersey to Ohio, and once my siblings and I glimpsed the farms and rolling hills, we heckled Ohio as Hicktown, USA. I didn't take the transition well. I cried longingly for the East Coast, but my mother constantly reminded us of the trade-offs: lower taxes, less pollution, and a slower pace of life, all of which were like foreign currency to me. I resented the golden cornfields and ambrosia sunsets because they came with long looks at church and in grocery stores. When cousins visited from Atlanta, Los Angeles, or New York, they teased us, asking if we spent our time cow tipping and wondering where all the other brown folks were.

"Don't you just admire the Amish?" my mother would say when we were out and saw them on the road. "They live lives of simplicity. Don't you envy that?"

I watched the clopping horses and rolling buggies as we passed them in our minivan and my mother smiled out the window. I flatly replied, "No." But in my head, I thought of one commonality we had with the Amish: we didn't belong on that road either.

Anger started early. I guess it was born from the constant friction—perpetually standing out with raven hair and mahogany skin, parents with accents, and a culture of familial centricity that swung far from the Western notions of individuality.

In grade school, I sputtered when I was angry, like a rusty faucet that couldn't believe it had finally been turned on. There were always those white boys I couldn't breathe around—the ones who pulled their eyelids toward their ears until they were razor thin and called me a chink when I passed them in the hallway. "Why don't you go back to your own country?"

And when my mom packed thermoses of Filipino lunches— jasmine white rice mixed with warm pork adobo or picadillo

with olives—there were smug white girls with PB&J sand-
wiches who called my food dogshit and embarrassed me to the
point that I asked my mom to stop packing me Filipino food.
Assimilation was survival. I learned how to code-switch, strad-
dle cultures, and create impenetrable borders: the lunch table
was for American food only and the dinner table was where I
could feast on steaming pillows of rice with *nilaga, kaldereta,* or
Spam. At home, there was my dad uproariously laughing on
long-distance phone calls to the Philippines with Sinatra re-
cords playing in the background. At school, I learned to feign
misunderstanding, roll my eyes, or swallow my anger.

On a particularly emotional night, after begging my mom to
let me stay home from school, she gave me a pastel diary with
a golden lock and key. Those early diaries, filled with loopy
cursive, reveal the beginnings of a girl negotiating rage, desire, and borders. It was the only place I could share what I
was experiencing. It became normal to yearn for what I could
not have: an escape route that led me to safety, where coming
of age didn't mean coming of pain. I associated all the ignorance and cruelty with place—a literal state, not state of mind.
I blamed Ohio.

Growing up, intolerance took on so many forms—misogyny,
anti-Asian sentiment, ignorance, white supremacy, settler co-
lonialism, model minority myths, sexism, exoticizing, fetishiz-
ing, tokenism. I was invisible yet hyper-visible. In Ohio, I was
an enigma to a lot of people and endured years of ignorant

questions about brown Asian identity. "Aren't all Asians the same?" "Are you a foreign exchange student?" "How do you speak English so well?" And all the while, even though I hated its presence, anger was always a companion. Wherever you walk, the sky is above you; wherever I went, anger was with me. My cheeks flushed, my heart pounded, the hairs on my arms rocketed to the sky, and I even grew lightheaded when I was outnumbered by white aggressors.

In the religious household and schools I was raised in, I was taught that anger was dangerous because of its proximity to hostility, violence, malice, and hate. Anger in and of itself wasn't wrong, per se, but wrath, a close cousin, was one of the seven deadly sins. It was difficult to coexist with anger.

So, when I finally could, I left.

I moved to the Pacific Northwest, then Boston, then New York—and experienced different forms of intolerance in all the famed big, fancy cities we are told are the hotbeds of free thought. It was different, but the same. There was much more representation and food options, and blending into crowds was easier, but there was a nagging similarity wherever I lived or traveled. In each place, I learned how whiteness and supremacy morphed, customized by region, population, and politics. Even during months-long stays in other countries like Nicaragua and even my ancestral home, I learned that my identity as a Filipino American meant different things in different places. In the Philippines, identity is much more stratified.

Punishments and rewards are based on body size, citizenship, language fluency, formal education, religious affiliation, and class. I was always searching to wholly belong to one place, but that isn't what I found. Instead, I found parts of myself everywhere I went, and learned I could adapt to a number of places.

By 2016, after living in so many different locations and moving in and out of Ohio five times, my life partner, Nick, and I chose to leave New York City to live in Columbus with our two children, for financial reasons and for family support. After living in Cincinnati (just a bit too contentiously Southern for comfort) and Cleveland (too much lake-effect gray and snow), Columbus—rumored to be a progressive haven with a decent food scene and queer-friendly politics—appeared to be a much-needed middle ground. I grunted over the moving boxes but hoped that since we were living in a blue county, we'd be with other folks who would celebrate the first woman president. The "grab 'em by the pussy" tape was playing on a loop and Ohio was polling for Hillary. I reminded myself that no presidential candidate in recent times had won the presidency without winning Ohio. As long as the Buckeyes went blue, the country would go blue.

A month before the election, during a long weekend, I drove from Columbus to Washington, DC, savoring the luxury of a quiet car without children and drinking in the changing landscape. Ohio flashed by like a silent movie and America was the story. The urban faded into pastoral scenery. As I inched along southeast Ohio, the intuitive alarm that often sounds before I enter hostile territory began to go off in my head. There were enormous banners, MAKE AMERICA GREAT AGAIN strewn from husk to husk along the sides of cornfields and TRUMP/PENCE 2016 staked into the ground. It was no surprise that southeast Ohio was Trump country, but the visual blast felt different from what I had seen before. When I left Columbus, I was certain Hillary would win, but what I saw on that drive convinced me otherwise. Ohioans were rising up for Trump and their anger was palpable. It was clear to me that Trump had Ohio, and if Trump had Ohio, he had the presidency. When I shared this realization with my coastal friends and activists, they tilted their heads in disbelief. They repeated the same thing over my insistence: "There's just no way, Lisa. There's no way he's going to win."

But as we know, for white men, there's always a way.

After the 2016 election, Ohio grew into a new political and personal battleground unlike what I had experienced before. But this time it wasn't just me. It seemed most people I knew were fumbling with personal and familial relationships because of political differences that created gashes or reopened old wounds. The political climate welcomes all kinds of anger now, and the most pronounced difficulty I've witnessed people experience is the inability to withstand anger's longevity, which is a prerequisite to reap its benefits. Most folks are only familiar with anger as explosive, uncomfortable, and destructive, which is only a fraction of anger's identity. There's more. There's a lot more to anger than that.

Living in the constancy of anger was, at first, difficult, because I bought into the idea that anger was, in and of itself, an unnatural state—the opposite of who I wanted to be: a consciously centered worker and writer for liberation. I also feared that the profundity of my anger would annihilate my chance to experience genuine joy. As it turns out, though, anger wasn't the problem; it was the suppression of it and not understanding it well enough to know how to express it. Prolonged anger can distill into a fuel for creativity, resistance and, ultimately, deliver moments of that elusive joy and a sense of belonging. But before it could transform into those things, I had to wear it and grow it to understand it as more than just a part of my narrative but also who I am as a person.

When anger is known only as an obstruction, the automatic reaction is repellant and removal. We end up repeatedly questioning who or what should be abandoned—do you sever old friendships because of how they voted? Do you visit family less because Fox News permeates their house? Do you leave home and move as far away from Ohio as you can?—instead of asking what is worth keeping.

Anger often leaves novices flailing. It's the inability to withstand the fire that causes the rush to judgment and frenzied journeys to the coasts of like-minded safety. For me, living in Ohio means living in opposition, and anger has constructed an advanced arsenal of weapons that allows me to move in the world, stay in relationships, and prioritize my well-being. Ohio forced me to coalesce anger with a sustainable lifestyle. Safeguarding my headspace and emotional bandwidth became a practice. I ask for more information before agreeing to participate in anything—organizations, school meetings, worship spaces, literary events, community dinners, and creative projects. I've become selective about which disagreements are worth pursuing ("Am I arguing with this person to deepen the relationship or deepen my point?") After almost forty years of fury, you learn that anger means organizing, not just mass movements but also the seemingly mundane details of daily life. But, even with all the prep work, there's no guarantee of emotional, psychological, or physical safety, and that awareness means taking nothing for granted.

I always have the option to move again, to escape into a slightly less dystopian reality, but the veneer of progress or liberalism quickly wears thin to reveal that I'm still in the same house, just peering out a different window. Regardless of region, the fight continues for women and LGBTQIA communities, voting rights, affordable housing, universal health care, and living wages. The fight, always, continues. We're all living in an Ohio—a state of ongoing tension.

When we drive on Highway 62 and pass the Confederate flags and the billboards declaring "one man, one woman =

real marriage," I see it now as an opportunity to give my kids what I wish I always had: an example of how to embrace anger; how to use it as a natural resource, whether facing injustice or critically interpreting political and religious propaganda. "You see these big signs?" I ask my kids when we pass religious billboards. "There's a lot of people out there who are afraid of anything different from themselves. People who are afraid will try to tell you who to love, how to love, or who to be friends with, but we're not afraid of other people just because they may be different from us. That's not who we are."

I tell my kids that anger is part of a well-stocked arsenal, and that the arsenal isn't just for Ohio. It's for life. Increasing scientific evidence shows trauma and pain can be physically, molecularly passed down from one generation to the next. I believe other things can be passed down, too. Although fear and habitual submission may have played a part in my formative years, I believe that having an alchemist as a mother—a person who learned how to transform caustic racist experiences into an arsenal for protection and healing—will extend some of my tools for living with anger to my children.

It's because of my choices that I can fluidly speak about anger as a source of strength, and how, even after all these years, I'm still challenged to define my identity as I teach my kids, and others, how to cultivate their arsenal, how to live with anger as an invitation to a life of resistance and relationship. Without anger, I would have never found like-minded women of color thinkers, writers, scholars, and activists in the bourgeoning landscape of the internet and social media. Without anger, I would not have had the fuel to examine and recognize the historical marginalization of other communities of color, especially Black women who have largely carried the burden of and endured the legacy of America's racist misogyny.

At so many points, I swore my anger would drive me out of Ohio, but because I befriended anger as a discovery site of necessary ferocity and growth, I now see Ohio as a particular kind of kiln, a place where I have learned that heat is the ingredient that solidifies clay into sculpture—into something of a marvel.

Crimes against the Soul

SHERYL RING

I usually wear skirts or dresses, with high heels and my hair done and nails polished. I love sparkles and makeup, and I usually wear lots of both. And though I haven't been blessed with the biggest chest in the world, it's decent enough. All in all, when I show up, it's not *that* hard to figure out that this person in front of you wearing makeup and sparkles and a dress with red hair down to her back is a woman. At the very least, I know I don't exactly scream "guy."

And yet I still get called "sir." And "him." And "he."

For a long time, I thought it was me, that I was being misgendered because I didn't pass well enough. We in the trans community have an awful habit of internalizing things like this. But the reality is, I *am* a woman, and therefore, I *am* what a woman looks like. *Every trans woman* is what a woman looks like. It's not that we all pass—it's that whether or not we "pass" is a question we shouldn't have to ask. We shouldn't need to meet some arbitrary patriarchal standard of womanly appearance in order to be referred to as the women we are.

We shouldn't, but we do.

My entire life has been a war between the woman I've always known I am and the man I was always told I was. Until I transitioned, I didn't recognize my reflection in the mirror; there was this sort of disassociation, a disconnect between who I was and what I saw. My mind couldn't process the idea that that was me (because it wasn't). There were the nights I cried, praying to God that He correct this mistake and fix me. There were the nights I cried, cursing God for giving me a body that mocked me every time I looked in the mirror. And then there were the nights I denied God existed at all, for no benevolent deity would do this to a person. My genitals were a tumor to be excised, a cancer to be cured. And some nights I cried myself to sleep, thinking myself insane.

I kept my identity a dark secret, terrified of what I was, until I could hide it no longer. The scariest step I ever took in my life was deciding to trust my mind and my heart over the people around me and the body that they saw. I came out after a bad car accident, one I was lucky to walk away from, because I realized that the thought of dying with people thinking me a man was too painful to bear. I would rather die a woman than live one more day as a man.

The truth is that not one of us *asked* to be trans, and most of us wouldn't have chosen it if we had been given the opportunity. My soul didn't ask for this body.

But I'm here, now, and this is how I was made. It's not my fault that I was born into a body that you can't see as female. If you could see my soul, you'd have no doubt. But when I tell you—when I expose a bit of my soul to tell you that, no, this body is wrong, and you in turn say it's my *soul* that's wrong, it's literally a soul-crushing experience.

To purposefully misgender someone is to commit an act of violence. It's the exercise of control over their person and identity without their consent.

The line between misgendering and sexual assault is blurrier than it might seem. I once went to a doctor's office where a nurse consistently misgendered me while checking me in. And then, without permission, she reached out and poked my breast, repeatedly, laughing all the while, because she wanted to see if it was *real*. (It is.)

By taking away my womanhood by misgendering me, she'd given herself permission to assault me. If I'm not a woman, then she can't be doing anything wrong by touching my breasts. Misgendering is a violation of my womanhood, just like grabbing my breast is. Its goal is the same: to put me in my place.

To misgender me is to take that femininity that I've nurtured and cherished and sustained in the darkest places—and which has nurtured and cherished and sustained *me* in the darkest places—and crush it. To deny its existence. And worse, deny its worthiness to exist. When someone misgenders me on purpose, they are saying I'm not woman enough to be recognized. They are saying that I'm not a woman at *all*—that I'm crazy, and they know me better than I know myself. When this happens, I feel my anger as pain. It's not in any physical part of my body, but I can feel it all the same, in a visceral way, somewhere deep, like being punched in the heart. I grit my teeth, I breathe heavier. I talk slower, and my voice becomes softer but with a sharper edge. The feeling of anger at being misgendered is the feeling of controlling my anger; of staying sweet and acceptably feminine in the face of being told I'm not.

I get misgendered everywhere. In the grocery store (I've had clerks refuse to give me deli meat unless I explain how a trans person is allowed to get a job), in restaurants (I had a manager literally try to break down the door to the women's restroom I was in), in doctors' offices (my favorite was a nurse telling me "you're not trans, you're just a drag queen").

Some of it comes from other lawyers. When I first came out, people who worked for the Attorney Registration and Disciplinary Commission (ARDC), the attorney licensing board in Illinois, told me I couldn't transition because it would be "deceptive" to the public. Then they made me deadname myself (use my birth name) in court for months. I would show up, in my dress and heels and makeup, and have to use my deadname in court arguments and on filings. When I petitioned to have this rule changed, they sent me a terse letter saying that because no other states allowed trans attorneys to use their chosen names, even legally changed names, they wouldn't either (that's not true, by the way).

I eventually decided, for the sake of my sanity, to use my legal, feminine name—my *real* name—anyway. Some attorneys refused to speak with me after that, saying they wouldn't violate an ARDC ruling by using female pronouns or my legal name.

When I came out, my boss refused to call me "she" or "her." He would call me "he" and "his" and "him" in court, in front of clients, and interrupt me to tell people to use male pronouns. When I asked him to use female pronouns for the umpteenth time, he told me, "I have a business to run, and I don't have time to coddle your feelings." When I insisted, he responded, "You didn't consult me in your decision to transgender, so I don't have to deal with your transgender issues." He fired me later that week, telling me, "I think you had a sex change just so you could be a bitch to me."

That statement, calling me a bitch, was the closest he ever came to calling me a woman unprompted.

After I found a new job, which wasn't easy with one firm after another unwilling to hire a trans lawyer, I was in court arguing a case before a judge who utterly refused to use female pronouns. I corrected him once, twice, three times. After the fourth time, he looked over at me and said, "I'm wearing the robe, so I can call you whatever I want." In that one conversation, the judge both negated my entire identity and forbade me from doing anything about it—I can't be a litigator if I'm not in judges' good graces. I felt brutalized, violated, put on a stage for the judge's amusement. I felt inhuman.

I wanted to lash out, to cause the same hurt I felt, but that just made it worse because then I was angry at myself for feeling that way. I felt guilty, because I was angry and women aren't supposed to be angry, and yet there I was. I felt exposed, vulnerable, like my inability to control my emotions was a personal failure. Then the anger gave way to humiliation—being forced to stand there, silently, trying not to show that I was on the verge of tears, knowing that if I were to challenge him, my career might very well be over. The judge forced me to choose between my dignity and supporting my family. The worst part of anger for me has always been when there's no outlet for it. For trans women, that happens all too often—especially when your livelihood depends on swallowing your anger.

More than once, I thought about quitting law. But one trans child, who had just started high school and wanted to be a lawyer one day, asked me to stay. "I need to know it's possible to be myself and be a lawyer," they told me. "If you leave, I'll have to bear the burden of being the first. And I don't think I

could do that." So, I take the body blows so the next generation doesn't have to.

As word got around, attorneys learned they could use my
gender as a weapon. And they did. I had an attorney call me
"that" and "it" in arguments. I had another refuse to speak with
me on a religious objection and ask the judge to order my cli-
ent to hire someone else. Another told me that I was required,
under the rules of civility, to allow him to misgender me because, as he put it, "it's easier for you to just let me call you a
man than it is for me to unlearn sixty years of morals." One
attorney sent me an email telling me that my presence in the
case was unfair to him because he didn't like trans people and
that he wouldn't discuss the case with me or agree to extend
professional courtesies unless I detransitioned. "You're either a
man or a woman," he said. "Grow up and face the real world."

These people substitute their judgment for mine, telling
me I don't get to control my body. Or they insist that they
know my identity better than I do. There's the "you're just a
gay man" argument. Well, no, I'm a lesbian, I'm exclusively at-
tracted to women (most of all my beautiful wife). Then there's
the "you're not a lesbian, you have a penis" argument, which
makes me wonder whether they inspect everyone else's genitalia and how they know what genitalia I have anyway. Both of
those usually come from the same person, which means they're
deciding my gender identity *and* sexuality for me. How gener-
ous of them. I really didn't need the help, though.

Then there's the argument that the sexism I experience isn't fair to cis women. I face sexism like any other woman. I get called "baby" and "honey" and "sweetheart." I have a halfway decent figure, a good pair of legs, and Julianne Moore hair, so I get hit on sometimes, usually in entirely inappropriate situations. I'm not thrilled about it, but it's a fact of life, so I deal with it.

A while back, a woman saw me get called "honey" by a guy who hit on me while I was at work. This woman came over to me and said, "It's so unfair how you face sexism like this. I get when it happens to me—but can't they tell you're not a woman? And why do they hit on you? You don't menstruate!"

In other words, she was offended that a guy found me attractive. Offended because I wasn't enough of a woman to be found attractive by a man.

There's this belief in transphobic circles that trans women can't be women because womanhood somehow depends upon reproductive capabilities. That argument hurts me the most. I'd trade just about anything—my sight, by hearing, my arms, my ability to *walk*—to be able to menstruate. I'm a woman, approaching thirty, and I can't get pregnant. I can't have kids of my own. *Thank you* for reminding me of that particular pain—I wonder if you tell all infertile women that they're men.

It's not a feeling, or a whim, or a curiosity that makes me a woman. It's who I am, and who I've always been. What I have—what I was born with—is a birth defect. No more and no less. Some people are born with a cleft palate. Some people are born conjoined. I was born into a body with the wrong parts. It happens. Nature isn't perfect.

But being trans is the *only* birth defect where we tell people who have it that they are delusional about it. If doctors told patients with cleft palate that they were *supposed* to be that way, they'd lose their licenses.

To misgender another purposefully is to commit an act of violence. But it's also an act of erasure. Erasure of identity, of presence, of existence. Saying that I am a man means I don't exist, because I am not a man and never will be. So the anger that comes from being misgendered is more than righteous indignation. It's a burning hatred against someone who would deny my very existence.

For Women Who Grew Up on Eggshells

MINDA HONEY

The night before my middle sister's wedding, my father sent me a text message. He wanted to talk, "So, it won't be awkward tomorrow." My father had not spoken to me for one year and two months. In this time, I had quit my job and moved from Denver, Colorado, to Riverside, California, for graduate school. I had learned my mother had leukemia. I had turned thirty. None of these occasions had warranted a phone call from my father or a text message or a flock of homing pigeons with apologies and congratulations and consolations secured to their miniscule ankles.

So, I spoke to someone else. As a graduate student, I was entitled to five free sessions a year with a therapist through the campus mental health clinic. I had never spoken to a therapist before, but when my sister called me that May to see if it'd be possible for me to fly home in June for her short-notice nuptials, I knew she was also asking me to stand in the same room as my father and smile. It would not be possible for me to return to Louisville, Kentucky, for her intimate thirty-person wedding without seeing him. And I did not know how to be in one city and leave my anger in another.

They didn't have any Black women therapists on campus, so I took an appointment with whomever was next available. The therapist was a white man in his fifties, probably around the same age as my father. His features were about as interesting as his university-issued office décor: faded teal couch, grayed-out walls, boxy desk, fluorescent lights. I would have preferred a warmer color palette with softer lighting, but this was the aesthetic of free mental health care. The therapist asked me why I was there, and I told him, "I'm either crazy now and need help or I will be by the time I get back from Louisville."

I wanted to talk about my father, the therapist wanted to talk about my mother. *My father is not speaking to me. My father can be cruel. My father has a temper.* But what about your mother? *My mother? My mother has cancer.*

Growing up, my mother taught us three girls how to read our father's moods like the weather, how to discern their ever-shifting winds. How to carve out a childhood at the base of an active volcano. How to survive the flash flood that was my father's temper, rage like water rising fast. He'd yell, he'd berate, he'd snarl. He'd snatch sentences from our mouths before we could finish them and twist them against us. This was at home. This was at school. This was without notice. This was a torrential downpour on a day the weatherman hadn't even warned me to bring an umbrella. There was so much of him that there became very little room for me in my own head. It never occurred to me to stand up to him, to raise my voice in return, find out what he was truly capable of. All I knew was what my mother had taught us, that you can't control the weather.

We rode the waves of his anger, never really knowing how far away from shore and safety we'd be swept. Every chair we neglected to push in after dinner, every light left on when leaving the room, every smear of egg yolk remaining on a counter was taken as a personal slight against him. Expressions, words, behaviors that seemed benign could mean something entirely different to my father, something worthy of a vortex of anger.

But the weather wasn't always in climate. He also helped us with our homework. Patiently explaining algebra to me, long hours spent solving for the unknown. He bought me a used car at sixteen and when I totaled it, he arrived at the scene unconcerned about the vehicle, saying, "All that matters is that you're okay," and replaced it with a brand new, cherry-red Jetta a few months later. I was born two months premature, and he often told me stories about holding me in the palm of one hand. How he'd dreamt of the father he lost at eight every night of his life until there was me. How I'd changed everything, meant everything to him.

This was our normal. A father who loved us, who clothed and fed us, who told us we'd never want for anything, but who left us starved for understanding. My mother taught us not to ask him for things when he was tired. Not to try to reason with him when he was raging, to let him cool down. Hours later, I'd write him letters and slip them under his bedroom door. The page was the only place I could be honest and free. Sometimes, my father would emerge from his room and behave as if nothing had happened. There'd be no apologies, maybe I'd be presented with a gift later that would be seemingly unrelated to his behavior. How I felt about these interactions was unimportant; I was the child. And I grew up to be a woman who never forgot the feeling of eggshells beneath her feet.

I performed the same delicate dance my mother taught me with all the men I dated. I weathered their emotions, I scoured their words for subtext and read their expressions as intently as a palm reader following the lines in a hand to some fictional finite end.

In Denver, I dated a man who lived one floor beneath me. We were dating, but we were *not* together, he insisted. We'd spend six nights straight together, all initiated by him, but if I pointed out we were essentially in a relationship, he'd do the hard work of staying away for a night. When drunk, he liked to plead with me to have his babies. But in the sobering light of morning, he'd panic at the thought of me taking his foolish requests seriously. For months, I stayed because there were also the romantic dinners, the chill nights on the couch, and the belief that beneath all his bullshit the feelings he had for me were real. With men, I knew only the reward in patience and how to sustain myself on what could be. As I had done with my father, I suspended the thoughts in my mind about who I was and what I liked or didn't like, to keep these men in my life.

But as I neared thirty, I began to question the way I'd been raised. I was trying to chart my own emotions, be my own weather pattern. So, when I saw the man I'd been dating, whose misery I'd been company to, chatting up another woman at a bar near our apartment complex, I approached him and tapped him calmly on the forearm. He shifted his attention from her to me long enough to blast me with a dismissive look. There in that moment, I knew the appropriate reaction was a downpour of rage. That *this* was the part of the movie where I sloshed a drink in his face or howled a warning at the woman, "He ain't shit!"

But I wasn't prepared to behave that way. I stopped seeing that man. It became apparent that it wasn't possible for me to both let my feelings be my guide and be in relationships with men that were possible only if I suppressed my emotions.

But then, what about my father? Was it possible to continue to have a relationship with my father, the man whose anger had silenced me for decades, while also demanding more from the other men in my life? Could I demand more from my father too?

When I was a kid, my father was obsessed with taking us to the Grand Canyon. For him, it represented some sort of peak parenting moment, but us kids couldn't have cared less about going. He'd pouted and finally let his dream go. "I wish someone had wanted to take *me* to the Grand Canyon when I was your age."

So, when a work-related road trip was going to bring me as close to this Wonder of the World as I'd ever be, I invited my father to drive out from Kentucky and join me. When we finally arrived at the Grand Canyon, my father refused to leave the parking lot. We'd had more than one tense conversation on the way, unable to find our new groove as two adults instead of as child and father. "Are you sure? We're already here," I asked him. He crossed his arms and looked away from me.

A younger me would have been so racked with concern over the consequences to come that she would have cut the entire trip short. But this was the adult me, the me who had been out of his house for more than a decade. The me who was financially free. Not the me he could cradle in a single palm or threaten to take her car away or expect to shrivel under the boil of his anger. This me declined to tell him about my writing when he asked, made it clear she was uninterested in hearing about his dating life, and did not hesitate to opt out of any other topics of conversation she didn't care to discuss. I had allowed the weight of my own feelings to crush the eggshells beneath my feet.

So, I left him behind and moved forward. I snapped selfies with the incomprehensible canyon yawning in the background beneath me, alone. One large single cloud hung in the blue sky, casting a soft gray cloud-shaped shadow on the otherwise vibrant view. An easy metaphor.

At the hotel that night, my father started an argument with me. As he had done at breakfast the previous day, he asked me about my writing. He wanted to know what I was writing about him. The truth? Nothing. It hadn't even occurred to me that he should play such a large role in the story of who I was as to appear on the page alongside the men of my love life. "I'm not writing about you. I'm writing about sex!" I shouted.

"Oh," my father said. "That doesn't bother me. I'm a very open person."

"What does that have to do with *me?*" I wanted to know. The question doubled over on itself. Even in a world created of my own words that did not feature him, he thought his feelings should override my own. I didn't keep my writing from my father because I had anything to hide, but because I wanted to protect what was most precious to me from him.

The next morning, he packed up and left before I was out of bed. Over the phone, he made it clear that I was not to call him. "I never want to speak to you again," he said. If only that had been the first time my father had ever uttered those words to me, maybe I would have felt remorse over the fine powder of eggshells beneath my feet. Maybe I would have let him be a cloud over my canyon. But it wasn't the first time, it was just the longest he'd ever meant it.

At the wedding venue, I got into an argument with my mother mild enough that it mattered to no one but her. I barely exchanged smiles with my father but agreed to meet him for lunch the next day. As I got into his car, he asked me how I was.

"Angry," I said.

"What? Why?" he asked, looking genuinely confused.

"Because you haven't spoken to me in over a year for no good reason."

"Well, I can't dwell on the past, I can only move forward."

"I didn't deserve to be treated that way."

"No one deserves to be treated that way."

It was like being in the car with "Big Mouth Billy Bass" shooting prerecorded one-liners at me but far less entertaining. I wanted my father to acknowledge what he'd done and how he'd hurt me. Back and forth we went like this until we arrived at the lunch spot and had bland conversation over even blander chain-restaurant Mediterranean food.

Back in Riverside, after the wedding, I returned to see the therapist one last time. He didn't actually smirk when I told him it was my mom I ended up fighting with at the wedding and not my father, but he might as well have.

"How can I be better around my parents?" I asked him. I knew I'd never be the daughter who's best friends with her parents, but surely we could address whatever deficit in me wouldn't allow me to be in the same room as them without getting emotional.

"I don't like to say this," the therapist said, but he said it anyway. "There's nothing wrong with you."

He shared a story about his own father, the way the man got under his skin over something as benign as telling him to sit down while he eats. "I know he's going to say it and that it's going to annoy me and we can avoid the whole thing by me just sitting down before he says anything, but the thought of doing that makes me angry too." Sometimes, this is just the way of parents and children.

Over the next year, I moved home to Louisville. My father and I had an off-and-on relationship. He took me to dinner for my birthday, and I cried fast-rolling tears over my meal in the small, cramped restaurant over how broken we felt.

"You're making people uncomfortable," my father said, seeing people at other tables shooting their eyes over at us and then back at their dining companions.

"I don't care about their feelings. I want you to care about mine," I said, continuing to cry until the server had the sense to bring our check so we could leave.

Outside the restaurant, we talked about why every disagreement or uncomfortable conversation ended with him shoving
me out of his life for months on end. That night, I found the
limitations of conversation. I flooded him with my angry words
like lava racing across the land to be comforted by the sea. And
still I was not satisfied. I raged, and I raged about the way he'd
treated me over the years. He kept returning to the fact that
at least he'd been there; for him the good outweighed the bad
and for me the bad was still worthy of his repentance. Now, I
was the active volcano and he was the one with the words that
were always wrong.

Sitting outside that restaurant, I felt the cold iron of the
patio chair through my clothes like the truth settling over me:
I knew that my father was never going to be more than who
he was. He'd told me the story of my birth so many times, how
holding me in his palm had changed him, that I had truly believed that who I am could change who he is.

I'd been searching for an answer about whether or not he
was a man I could have in my life, when the question that
needed an answer was whether it was fair for me to continue
to be in my father's life for the sole purpose of berating him for
who he had been and for who he was? For my own sake and
his, I needed to accept him for the good and the bad or move
forward without him.

That night, I began to understand that there's a difference
between someone actively trying to harm you and someone's

specific constellation of shortcomings being harmful to you. It's the difference between an earthquake, inescapable and unanticipated, tearing everything you've built down and stepping into the path of a tornado even as the sirens ring out their warning. What I'm saying is that unlike when I was a child, I now had a choice, I too had power over our relationship.

I'd spent my whole life ceding ground in relationships to men and letting them dictate the terms. If my father couldn't be who I wanted him to be, or even who I needed him to be, he could still be worthy of my love, but I was the one who got to decide what that love looked like.

My father is making an effort to be better. Maybe because he knows the time he spent not speaking to me after the Grand Canyon taught me I could withstand a world without his love and taught him he could not withstand a world without mine.

Now, he plans lunches and arrives on time. He weeds my yard in ninety-degree weather and sprays around the windows of my home to keep the bugs out. His apologies come easier, he retreats more readily when he comes up against my boundaries.

Recently, he called me. "When the weather cools down, let's do the walking bridge twice a week." He paused, then, "I'm trying to be a better father."

"I'm thirty-three," I said. Accepting my father as he is means refusing to join him in chasing after the fantasy of who he believes he can or should be. I won't sit on top of the stack of unachievable expectations he's burdened our relationship with and then rage at him when his knees buckle, when he inevitably lets me down. I refused the new terms he was presenting.

I told him I couldn't commit to that, I couldn't take on the obligation of it. He told me to look at it as an opportunity, to just think about it. I could already feel my temper prickling up. What was driving him to continue this cycle of dreaming too big, disappointing me, and then disappearing on me? I want us to come to a place where our relationship is stable and static, where all the questions have been answered. I'm tired of renegotiating our roles in each other's lives. Every time he tries to begin the cycle anew, it sparks up all of my feelings from the past. And anger is the only thing I've found to squelch out the feelings of helplessness that I felt as a child.

My father didn't call me again after that conversation. I know it's on me this time to call him, but I let weeks go by because I am without the right words to say. It's me and my anger in this place between a canyon and a bridge.

My father has mellowed with age. He's different with me. But I'm. Still. Angry. And I don't know where to put that anger. It doesn't feel good when I put it on him and doesn't feel right when I sit with it. And if this anger isn't my fault, why am I the one burdened by the weight of it? Why won't it just dissipate? And now the anger is joined by guilt that I can't indulge him by playing a do-over dress-up game with the past, him as the infallible role-model father and me starring as the doting daughter. I need to find a way for peace to exist between us without either of us pretending to be something we aren't. Because even if anger does, fathers don't live forever.

No More Room for Fear

MEGAN STIELSTRA

"Mom, I have a question," said my ten-year-old son. I like ten. I like the conversations we have about the world, although truth be told I am having a hard time with the world right now. I'm having a hard time understanding it, let alone explaining it, and I find myself wishing for him to be three again, when his biggest question was why I wouldn't let him jump off the balcony. Our apartment was three stories above Lawrence Avenue and the balcony had one of those slide-y glass doors, which I padlocked like a bank vault. My little boy would press his palms against the glass and say, *Mommy, let me out*, and I'd be like, *My ass you're going out there*, and he'd say, *But I can fly!* and I'd squat down to his eye level and say, *Launching yourself off the balcony is not being kind to your body and, baby, we have to be kind.*

Was it ever that simple? *Be kind.*

"Mom," he said again. He was in the back seat. Somehow these conversations always happen on the way to school in the morning and it is not easy to navigate Chicago rush hour while finding an age-appropriate response to *What is a pee tape? What is treason? Who is Harvey Weinstein? What happened in Puerto Rico, in Flint, Las Vegas, where is Gaza, what's a bump stock, who is Laquan McDonald? They shot him how many times?* He counted to sixteen on his fingers and I cried.

I looked in the rearview mirror. His eyebrows were wrinkled up. Those eyebrows are mine. The face is his dad's. The mind is his own, a child's thoughts and questions in 2018 the year of our lord in this, our great American experiment.

"Mom," he said, urgent now—whatever this is, it's important—"What's a walkout?"

It was one month after the shooting at Marjory Stoneman Douglas High School in Parkland, Florida, and students and teachers across the country were walking out of their classrooms to raise awareness about the impact of gun violence. In a few hours, I'd be walking out of my own classroom at Northwestern, something my students and I had discussed the previous week, but I hadn't thought to ask whether there would be a walkout at my son's elementary school. My husband was out of the country that week for work, and I was trying to keep my head above water: my job, my deadlines, my beautiful, troubled city and this beautiful mess of a country, and the child I'm raising in both.

When he was seven years old—I will never forget this for as long as I live—we were in Oakland for Thanksgiving with family. He and his cousin were playing with squirt guns inside the house and my son asked if they could go in the front yard where there was more room. His cousin, who is Black, looked at his mother, who is Black, who looked at me—I am white—and we had a conversation without words that included centuries of American history and a lifetime of love.

My son and I went for a walk. We talked about Trayvon Martin. About Tamir Rice. We talked about whiteness and responsibility and criminal justice and gun violence. "These things are complicated," I said. "Even for grown-ups."

"I don't think it's complicated," he said. "You have to be kind."

"Look for the helpers," I told my son after Parkland, after Las Vegas and Santa Fe and Orlando and Sutherland Springs and Charleston and Chicago and Pittsburgh, but there are only so many times I can quote Mr. Rogers before I rip down the goddamn sky.

Here's something I haven't told him: in December 1993, my high school chemistry teacher drove home at the end of the day, grabbed one of his eleven guns, drove back to school, and opened fire at an administrative board meeting. My father was on that administrative board. Yes, I am lucky that he is still here, but it doesn't mean I'm not still haunted. Five hours I thought he was dead and twenty-five years I have carried that fear. It's in my body. It's in my bones. It's in my imagination: Whenever there's a school shooting, I see my dad hiding under a desk. I see the gunman pausing to reload. I see the blood.

After Columbine, it wasn't my dad anymore. It was me.

After Virginia Tech, it was my students.

After Sandy Hook, it was my son.

I pulled the car to the side of the road, turned to face my ten-year-old white American son, and told him about the ten thousand Latinx youth in East LA who walked out of their high schools to demand better learning conditions. I told him about the Children's Crusade in Alabama in 1963, when Dr. King was arrested and wrote "Letter from a Birmingham Jail." I told him about the Chicago Public School walkouts in 2013 after our dearly departing mayor presided over the largest school closing in history. "Walkouts are disruptive," I said. "And uncomfortable. Those things are necessary for change."

Then I did the most terrifying thing: I dropped him off at school.

Two hours later, I stood in the brutal cold with hundreds of students, staff, and faculty to commemorate the one-month anniversary of the shooting at Marjory Stoneman Douglas High School. At 10:17, there was a moment of silence for the seventeen people—fourteen students and three teachers—who were killed that day. Northwestern's president spoke. Then the mayor of Evanston. And then, one after another, students took the mic to tell stories of how their lives had been affected by gun violence—grief, fear, rage, hope.

I've been teaching creative writing for twenty years. I don't know if a story can save us—but it sure as hell can show us what's worth fighting for.

I wrote about this on the internet and some dude—it's always a dude—came into my DMs and said, "Stop making everything so fucking political," and, rest in peace, I killed him with my brain. You think *this* is political? This is what happened at work today, Dude. I would love to have written about the incredible class discussion I had with a bunch of brilliant writers about diction and syntax, narrative and reflection, Joan Didion and Toni Morrison, but we didn't have that discussion because we were walking out of our classroom, standing in the cold, and listening to young people try to save their own lives.

In retrospect, it was an excellent lesson on Morrison: "No time for despair," she wrote in *The Nation*. "No place for self-pity, no need for silence, no room for fear."

Two more hours later I was outside of my office, trying to find my keys. The Creative Writing Department at Northwestern is on the basement level of University Hall; our windows butt up against the ceiling and offer an excellent view of people's legs. My phone buzzed with a text message. I unlocked the door, turned on the lights, and read:

This is the Northwestern Emergency Notification System. This is not a drill. A person with a gun—

Outside my window, people were already running.

Like most teachers—and students, for that matter, starting as early as kindergarten—I have been through civilian active shooter training as designated by the Department of Homeland Security. The script for my particular situation goes like this: turn off the lights, lock the door, and get down— "shelter-in-place," it's called. I knew that the space underneath my desk couldn't be seen from the window or the hall. My office door has this narrow vertical window and on the day I moved in, I stood in every corner of the room to determine lines of visibility. I do this in my classrooms, too. Count exits. Test locks. Identify potential weapons: projector, laptop, chair. What about my body, a shield between my students and a shooter? What if the shooter was a student? When do you shoot a student? When do you take a bullet? Would I take a bullet? Would I cry? Would adrenaline kick in and I'd have that extra strength mothers get when they lift buses off their children?

I can't be the only teacher who thinks like this.

I pretzeled up underneath my desk, put my phone between my thighs, and stared at my inbox. Updates from the university came every twenty minutes: *police are responding . . . stay where you are*. Friends started to call as local news posted the story. When CNN picked it up, I texted my mother so she wouldn't worry, as if it's possible for a mother not to worry. I watched my students on various social media platforms, many of them reporting what was happening. They are writers, journalists— thorough and precise, poetic and ferocious. *I'm sorry the world is like this*, I wanted to tell them. *I'm proud that you're trying to make it better*, but I couldn't, I was holding my heartbeat, trying to control my breath the way my yoga teacher taught me, trying to control my thoughts the way my therapist taught me, trying to control my—not fear. This wasn't fear.

It was rage.

Twenty-five years I'd imagined this moment and every time I was panicked, shaking; now, instead, I was white-hot and clenched, my muscles seething. Psychologists have long written about anger as a secondary emotion to fear, but I could give a shit about theory. This was gut-level; my body, my bones. I should not be under a desk. My students should not be stacking chairs against the doors of their classrooms. We should not be teaching children to throw school supplies at an imaginary bad guy with a gun. My high school chemistry teacher should not have had eleven guns. The Parkland shooter should not have had *a* gun. He was nineteen years old. He'd been expelled for bringing knives to school. His mother had recently died. He made a comment on YouTube that he wanted to be a professional school shooter when he grew up and was reported to the FBI, who didn't do anything to help; he needed help, we need help, mental health services and anger management counseling and a couple generations worth of education and parenting to dismantle rape culture and toxic masculinity. It will be complicated and near impossible but we will do it because for the love of god we will make a better world, but to do that we need resources, *not firearms*.

I'd been under my desk for an hour when I got the message from my son's elementary school saying the police had put them on lockdown, too. At that point I could've exploded University Hall with the sheer force of my fury. I stared at the clock—a boiling kettle, a watched-fucking-pot—for another excruciating hour until an email popped up from Northwestern with the subject heading ALL CLEAR. I didn't read it, just grabbed my keys and rushed to my kid. There were 3.3 miles between us, Sheridan to Dempster, and a street full of double-parked cars and panicked parents.

Children are stronger than any of us, and mine in particular is tough as hell. That said, he'd spent two hours imagining that his mother was dead.

It's in *his* body now. *His* bones.

"Mom, I have a question," he said that night. We were in his bed, both of us exhausted. "Was anyone hurt?"

"No," I said. Reports were coming in about what had happened and I struggled to explain. "Someone called the university and . . . they made a joke."

"A joke," he repeated. His eyebrows wrinkled up. "It didn't feel like a joke."

"I know," I said.

"I'm sorry," I said.

"It's complicated," I said.

Except it's not complicated. It's not complicated at all.

"Were you—" he started, and I steeled myself for yet another conversation about violence, about our great American experiment. "Were you scared?"

I told him about the messages I'd gotten from friends. That I thought the people at my job handled it very well and I was grateful. That the young writers I work with were so smart and brave. "So many helpers!" I said for the hundredth time, and I started to say something about kindness, but he was already asleep.

I lay there for a while, listening to him breathe, thinking how long I'd been afraid of this day.

I don't have any more room for fear.

I am too fucking furious.

Going to War with Myself

KEAH BROWN

I am angry all the time. That's my secret. I am so angry. I often dream of confronting the people who remind me of my otherness, letting them see just how angry the woman they're so intent on watching limp can be. The fantasy version of myself prepares for war, fists clenched and heart beating fast. She is unfazed by the idea of consequence. I imagine my body turning red and steam coming out of my ears as I walk toward them. One foot in front of the other as I watch them squirm a little. When we're finally face-to-face, my normal color returns, but the anger remains. I tap my left hand on my left leg, keeping time as if I am singing a song and not screaming at them to get a life or a semblance of decorum, or that I am a human being.

When I was in high school, someone asked me through Formspring, the anonymous question platform, "Why are you a cripple?" It read less like a question and more like a statement, a way of saying, "You don't belong, in case you forgot." A way to let me know that they saw my disability no matter how desperate I was to appear unaffected by it.

I hate when people feel the need to remind me that I am other. They speak about my disability in such a negative way that it makes me feel less than human, and angry enough to flip a car or two. My disability, my Blackness, and my womanhood are seen before my humanity, my desires and dreams, if those are seen at all. Navigating that reality daily would make anyone question themselves after a while. I get angry at other people's ignorance now, but for a very long time my anger was directed at the wrong person: myself. Instead of giving the people who mocked my disability a piece of my mind like they deserved, I turned my barbs and insults inward. I thought that I alone was responsible for the way I existed in the world. Knowing I couldn't cure cerebral palsy simply fueled my disdain for myself.

I was so mortified, ashamed, and filled with anger after that Formspring question, I wanted to reach through my computer, grab the person who asked it, and repeatedly bang their head against my desk until I felt better. What I actually did was refuse to eat for the remainder of the day and cry myself to sleep, convinced I was a freak who didn't belong.

I spent hours in front of my mirror picking myself apart piece by piece, chastising myself for the way my voice sounded when I answered questions in class and how red my face got from crying in group therapy. Back then everything I did was worthy of ridicule, everything about me made me angry at myself. For years, I turned my anger into cuts; I made myself bleed because my anger was already red hot whenever I entered the world and someone made a mockery of my being.

My biggest fear in life was being a burden to my friends and family. I believed that if they knew how angry and sad my body made me, they would be angry at it too. I couldn't have us all hating me, I couldn't handle that kind of rejection from people I loved. So, I never said, "Hey, I hate myself because my disability makes me different and undesirable in the eyes of all the boys at school and will likely keep me undesirable for the rest of my life." I kept the hate and anger to myself.

Deep down, I knew I couldn't sustain waking up every single day feeling this way. So, I planned end dates for my life, convinced that everyone who knew me—and the world at large—would be better off. The life I lived was not a life worth living at all. A life of waking up every day and wishing to die, a life spent tearing myself down in the name of what I believed to be honesty. I was so unhappy that getting out of bed each day felt harder than any schoolwork could be. I was alive, sure, but I was not living. So, I prepared to die.

And then I lost my grandmother. When she died, I realized that it would have broken my grandma's heart to know how I was breaking my own heart every day with insults, anger, and sadness directed at me alone. Losing her was a wake-up call. I still hated myself, but her loss opened a little crack for the idea that maybe I shouldn't. After all, someone so lovely, so kind, and so giving loved me, so why couldn't I do the same?

Death was never what I truly wanted, I know that now. What I truly wanted was relief from all the pain and hurt the world caused me when it told me I would never be enough. The same pain and hurt I fed back to myself. Despite believing that my family would be better off, I did not really want to leave them. I didn't want to say goodbye to my mother's hugs, my sister's laughter, or my family's belief in being together in times of sorrow and joy. So, I stayed.

Eventually, things started going well for me professionally. My writing was published in larger publications like *espnW* and *Teen Vogue*. Publishing in these places helped me realize that I wanted to be alive to see things pan out. I put my worth in my work, and I started seeing that I had something to offer the world, a purpose to be here and survive in the face of rejection and mockery.

I walked into my bathroom one morning, with one sock on and one sock off, wearing pajama pants and an old oversized T-shirt. I caught a glimpse of myself in the mirror, and despite looking like your average groggy and messy-haired morning person, I was shocked to discover that I thought I looked cute. Now, I had had these thoughts before, but they were always fleeting and dismissed immediately. This, however, I could not dismiss. I thought it would fade with time, but it didn't. The thought woke with me again the next morning, climbing out of bed first and making its presence known before I even reached another mirror. I'd let myself feel purpose and value through my work, and it spread into the rest of my life until I was able to actually see myself—a cute Black woman with a round face, big eyes and a big smile, long fingers and arms, black hair, and big feet. A woman with promise and potential who isn't like anyone else and who knows now that she doesn't have to be to matter.

Of course, feeling cute a couple mornings in a row wasn't enough to banish the demons of self-hate and self-harm for good, but it helped me gather the courage to fight them head-on. I decided to work at happiness, to unlearn self-hatred. Inspired by that chance moment of appreciating my own reflection, I decided I would learn to love myself by saying four things I liked about myself out loud, every day. "I like my cheeks, I like my eyes, I like my loyalty and my sense of humor." I said these things as many times as it took to believe them, actively chasing negative thoughts away with positive ones; sitting with my accomplishments and joy, relishing in them. I still say new things now when I need the reminder. And I started taking more pictures of my face, so I could get used to the way it looked when I was genuinely happy.

I did this every day for a year, and I discovered more about myself than I ever thought possible. I have a cute nose, cute ears, and a loud laugh. I'm pretty good at telling my own stories, both real and imagined, and telling the stories of others. And I have the potential to grow from here.

As hard as I worked, I still struggled with setbacks and doubts, and I responded by isolating myself from everyone I loved. I'd refuse to discuss bad days or mood changes, because I was ashamed that these negative feelings had returned even momentarily. Whenever I felt myself getting angry at someone for mocking my disability, I felt guilty immediately after, chastising myself for being "weak" in my anger after I spent so long making it a harmful force in my life. To truly be happy, I thought, I had to banish anger from my life completely.

But denying myself my full range of emotion gave me anxiety, and I realized quickly that this was not sustainable. So, instead of trying to eradicate anger from my life, I began directing it at things I believed needed to be improved—causes I was already passionate about, where my anger could be fuel. My anger, I decided, could be used to call for better representation in media and entertainment for marginalized people. To do this, I started talking about it consistently in the places I knew my voice would be loudest: Twitter and my written work. I made Twitter threads about the effects of harmful representation of people with disabilities, and I have written extensively about not only my life as a disabled Black woman but also some of the hardships the disabled community as a whole faces.

I am angriest now when I think about the exclusion of disabled people in the conversations about inclusion and diversity, the rights we stand to lose under the current presidential administration, the deaths of disabled people at the hands of caretakers or family members that go mostly unreported. And about the treatment and desertion of Puerto Ricans after Hurricane Maria, the treatment of immigrants, and the growing list of Nazis, racists, transphobes, homophobes, and ableists finding power in today's America.

I used to feel mortified by the world's negative view of my disability and me, by association. Now, I believe in saying "fuck you" to anyone who has a problem with my otherness, differences, or my anger. I am great, I have nothing to be ashamed of. The shame should be theirs; the weight of their own prejudices and discriminatory behavior is no longer mine to bear.

I know that my anger is beautiful now, because I am beautiful too. Anger is necessary when it propels us toward equality, justice, righting historical wrongs, and action. We marginalized people deserve to be angry with so much at stake, despite the stereotypical and negative connotations behind our anger. I'd be concerned if we weren't. Now is not the time for rose-colored glasses; now, we fight and use our anger as a tool to remember who and what we are fighting for. Let your anger change the world for the better, because we can't wait for other people to be angry for us—we would be waiting our entire lives for that. I, for one, am excited to burn it all down and build it back up to be better than it ever was before.

So Now What?

ANNA FITZPATRICK

The night I was raped was also the night I got stuck in an elevator, a piece of symbolism so trite that I rolled my eyes when I
realized it the next day. I had ridden the elevator several floors
up before it stopped, the doors refusing to budge as I jammed
the "door open" button several times. Nothing was happening.
I started to panic, before pushing the ground floor button and
returning to the lobby. I was not as trapped as I first thought.
Later, my date would explain that the elevators in his condo
didn't go above a certain floor after a certain time of night.

   We'd had a short fling almost two years earlier, predicated
entirely on sex. A Tinder match, we had no friends in common and he was the exact opposite of me, which was a large
part of the appeal: outgoing, worked in tech, liked sports, no
interest in books, out almost every night of the week. He was
nice to me except when we fucked, which accounted for the
rest of the appeal. I liked it when he was rough with me. We
would talk about what was okay and what wasn't before and
after—boundaries, safe words, limits—and at least once he

stopped things during because "my head didn't seem into it." I told my friends how nice it was to find a partner who seemed to thoroughly understand consent and who could also throw me down.

Our brief tryst ended amicably; our schedules were different, it was hard to make plans, and we decided it was best to go our separate ways. Because I'm bad at ending things cleanly, we stayed in touch. I was almost always the one who texted him first, usually when I was drunk or couldn't sleep or was just plain horny. The exchanges happened on Snapchat, where messages could disappear as soon as they were sent. Sometimes we would sext, sometimes he would tell me he was busy. I was aware this gave him the upper hand, but the power dynamic was part of our foreplay. We knew our roles. It was all just a game.

We hadn't spoken in months and hadn't seen each other in over a year. He sent the first text, which was unusual. He was having a bad day, he said. He just wanted to have really rough sex. I understood the impulse, but I wasn't in the mood. "I'm on, like, day one of my period and am not feeling very sexy," I said.

"Cool, so just anal, got it," he replied.

"Haha. I'd be willing to give you a blow job, and that's it," I typed.

"Come over," he replied a few minutes later, along with his address. This was also unusual; he usually came to my place. It was already late. I took a cab.

He had been drinking, which was the first thing I noticed when he met me outside his condo door, once I had finally figured out the elevator. I had stopped drinking about a year prior, because, as I explained to my friends, "I feel like I always do dumb things when I drink that I regret the next day." The second thing I noticed upon seeing him was how much I missed him, specifically, how much I missed having sex with him. He told me about the hard time he was having; trouble at work, a friend who was in an accident. I told him I was sorry and asked what he wanted to do. He replied by kissing me.

He pinned me down on the bed, which was normal for us. He took off my clothes, which was normal for us. He flipped me on my hands and knees and hit me a few times, which was normal for us. I felt him spit on me, then finger me. I was confident he wouldn't try to have intercourse with me, as I'd already stated I didn't want to do that tonight. But then there was pressure. And a lot of pain. I was confused, a sense of disbelief, as I realized he was trying to have anal sex with me. *He wouldn't do that,* I told myself, as he continued to do just that. *This isn't happening because he wouldn't do that. I must be confused.* I was dead sober but didn't trust my immediate experiences. He hadn't even put on a condom, he had just gone for it. He pushed in farther. I started to yell.

"NO!" I shouted. I couldn't think of any other word in that moment. I was panicking, feeling like a kid who had just touched a hot stove. "No no no no no." He stopped and pulled out. "I have to go to the bathroom," I said quickly, before he had the chance to explain himself. I left the bedroom and sat on the kitchen floor by the fridge, arms around my knees, trying to process what had just happened.

Did I go into too much detail there? I have never really told the story in full, and part of me wants to make sure you get the full picture. I still feel an impulse to protect him. It's important for me that you know he was having a bad day. It's important to know that he did stop, eventually, when I said "No," even though I know he shouldn't have penetrated me in the first place. These are the details I obsessed over in the days, weeks, and months after.

Eventually, I went back to the bedroom, convinced I was overreacting. I spent the night. His alarm went off just after six the next morning. I was out of it, sleepy, "Can't we sleep in?" but he said he needed to get ready for work. He was solemn, quieter than usual, as I blinked myself conscious, remembered where I was, and suddenly felt a pain where he had penetrated me without any lubrication. I quickly got dressed as I mentally replayed the events of last night. I hugged him and kissed him goodbye, and started to walk home. Minutes later, my phone buzzed with a Snapchat notification.

"I'm embarrassed about what happened last night," he said. "I'm sorry."

I wanted to be cool and tell him it was no big deal, that I

was already over it, look at how chill and nonchalant I could be, let's hang out again soon. I took a deep breath.

"I believe you're sorry," I wrote back. "But maybe it's best we don't talk to each other anymore."

My mind oscillated obsessively between two thoughts: The first was that he had just made a mistake, that he misread the situation and immediately regretted it, and that I was being unfair. The second was that I never really knew him at all, that this was the person he really was, a person who liked to see how far he could push things during sex, to find out what he could get away with, that the only reason I hadn't noticed it before was because I had been game for anything, and that if I didn't say or do anything he would do worse things to other women and it would be all my fault. I wasn't sure what steps I was supposed to take next, or how I was supposed to feel, so I waffled in a state of suspension, trying to jam the "doors open" button on an elevator that wouldn't budge.

I had been in bad situations with men. I had been groped by strangers on the sidewalk, and repeatedly threatened with rape by an angry high school classmate after I turned him down for a date, and coerced into performing acts with a date that, though they might have been hard to argue under the legal definition of assault, left no doubt in my mind that the guy was an asshole. Those were men I already disliked, or were relative strangers, and it was easier for me to think of them as Bad People. I didn't feel the urge to defend them as I did this time around. I still guiltily thought of him with affection, especially the early time we had spent together.

My best friends talked me through it. "I mean, I went over to his place in the middle of the night to hook up, what did I *expect?*" I said.

"Yeah, but it still doesn't mean it was your fault," said one friend.

"He's just, he's normally such a good *person*," I told another.

"He can have been sincerely nice to you in the past, but his actions that night weren't the actions of a nice guy," they said.

They were patient with me. They knew I didn't want to demonize him, so they didn't either. They knew that I felt uncomfortable using the word *rape*, a word that was dramatic and criminal, that would posit me as a victim or a survivor when I didn't feel much like either. On a mental level, I *knew* better. I had held signs at Take Back the Night and the Women's March, I read and retweeted all the right think pieces about the ambiguities of sexual assault, I had held my own friends' hands when they had had similar experiences. But on a gut level, I kept fighting with myself. *Are you saying what happened to you is as bad as what happens to* real *victims? And if it was that bad, shouldn't you want justice? Shouldn't you want him to suffer?*

I told my therapist, "I just don't know what to *call* it. I mean, was it rape?"

She said, "You don't have to call it anything. Just focus on how you feel right now."

I felt angry, though I wondered if for the wrong reasons. I was angry that he had ruined what we had, that I could no longer text him, that I felt the need to defend him to my friends. I was angry that if I wanted to use the word that best fit the situation—*rape*—then I would feel myself pushed into a category that I wasn't even sure I belonged in. I felt failed, above all, by language and the lack of words available to me. To speak matter-of-factly about what happened felt glib. To analyze it felt indulgent. *It was a minute of your life,* I kept repeating to myself. *Why can't you just get over it?*

I was angry later, when I told other men about what had happened, future sexual partners and friends, and they replied with male bravado and grandstanding—"Want me to beat him up?" "He can't get away with this!"—that seemed to center their machismo over my feelings. I remained externally placid in these situations while these men were allowed to display unfettered emotion and it was my job to calm them down and tell them, "No, no, it's okay." And I was angry still when I joined in tweeting during the #MeToo movement, at having strangers in my mentions saying "I believe you" as if I was seeking their validation when I was just stating the facts about my life. I was angry because I, too, have told strangers I believed them, because women *are* so often disbelieved when stating the facts of their life, and because the language around sexual assault is so limited that eventually everything starts to feel like a platitude. Again, I would smile calmly and say "Thank you" when what I really felt was the urge to tell these polite strangers to fuck off. I was angry at the sleepless nights spent interrogating my own reactions, always, "You're overthinking it" or "Not enough," and I would lurk on his Twitter feed and see him updating his banal thoughts, business as usual. I was angry when I went to get an STI test, while waiting three months for the HIV test, and I was fucking pissed off when one of my other casual partners told me we should "hold off seeing each other" until I got the test results back. I told him he was being an asshole, the only time I expressed any anger during this time, and when he apologized the next morning, I swallowed my anger again and told him don't worry, it's no big deal, I'm already over it.

My anger was not a constant, all-encompassing presence, and so it felt like I had dealt with the problem as much as I could. It presented itself like a bruise on the shin, blended in with other emotions—almost easy to forget about, unless something bumped into it. I didn't think about it for days, and then burst into tears at a screening of Colossal when Jason Sudeikis's seemingly aw-shucks-nice-guy character gets drunk and lashes out at Anne Hathaway's aimless heroine. I felt on edge when a drunk man tried to cut me off on the sidewalk in broad daylight, a common occurrence that now left me feeling shaken and distracted for the rest of the day. At times my anger felt lacking, taking a back seat to a cloudy, ambiguous shame that quietly instructed me to shut up and let the women with the real stories talk, the ones with real PTSD, who had suffered real consequences from their assault. I was fine. My life was fine. So I had bad moods now and then; wasn't that just life?

I was angry when I read statistics about the number of rapists who actually go to prison, but I was also angry at the idea that I was supposed to *want* him to go to prison, as if putting a person through the carceral system was supposed to be some form of justice. I was angry at myself, then, for using my anti-prison politics to downplay the actions of a straight white thirty-year-old male sex offender. I was angry that I was being made to feel like a judge. When people asked me what I wanted to happen, I said, "I want for this not to have happened in the first place."

In her book *The Reckonings*, Lacy M. Johnson says of her own abuser, "I don't want him dead. I want him to admit all the things he did, to my face, in public, and then to spend the rest of his life in service to other people's joy." More pain creates more sorrow, she writes. I think often of the limited avenues provided for victims of sexual assault, even in more progressive spaces. We are supposed to be bloodthirsty, to want revenge, to find closure in the suffering of those who wronged us. The punishment of the assailant is prioritized over the healing of the survivor. I understand why some women want these things. At times, I find it a natural impulse. But my rage manifested differently; I was angry less at a person and more at a series of ambiguities, unsure of what to do beyond sitting around and stewing in my own helplessness. The moment had replayed in my mind so many times, alternating crystal clear and like a fuzzy videocassette.

Almost a year after that night, I had downloaded a new dating app on my phone. It was one of the ones where you can only message the other person if both of you have consented to the match. I had idly been scrolling through for half an hour when I saw his face. I froze. I hated his face. I missed him so much. I was tired of being angry. I hesitated. I swiped right. We matched immediately.

I had never blocked his number or his Snapchat, but he hadn't tried to contact me before this—I had told him not to, after all. He messaged me, to say he owed me an apology. He said he was so sorry.

I told him the truth—that I couldn't make up my mind whether he was a bad person or not, and that I didn't know if he had done this to other women as well.

"I've never forgotten that night," he said. "I've been much, much more careful since. I never want any other woman to feel how you did."

He could easily have been lying. I had dealt with men who would say or do horrible things and then come to me later, asking for forgiveness, promising it would never happen again, falling into a cycle. But he had left me alone when I asked him to. He wasn't seeking anything from me. And so I told him that it was good that he had thought so much about it. I told him it was good he felt bad if it meant he was more careful with women in the future. I told him I wanted to move on with my life. And I told him I forgave him.

Typing those words out was an experiment. I wasn't sure how much I believed it myself. It felt like I had downed a dozen shots of espresso rapid-fire, and up until that point of the conversation I couldn't really distinguish one emotion from another. Yet after hitting send, I was imbued with a sense of power. I wasn't absolving him from what he had done, but he would no longer be my responsibility. He had acknowledged his wrongdoing after nearly a year of occupying so much space in my head, and I was declaring myself ready to move on. It was a different, clearer sensation than the anger that had burrowed itself in my gut for the past year—not total relief, but gratitude that I gave myself permission to turn my thoughts away from what would and could happen to him, and instead focus on myself. I was able to sleep okay that night.

We haven't spoken since then—again, my choice. I told him I still didn't want to hear from him, and kept him blocked on all social media. I want to believe that people who have made mistakes—including horrible mistakes, at the expense of others—have the capacity to change, grow, and better themselves. My entire worldview is based on this belief. But it is not my job to personally rehabilitate the man who has hurt me.

In the last couple of years, as we've watched celebrities attempt to return to their cushy careers months after admitting guilt, much of the cultural conversation has revolved around, "What, so we're just never supposed to move on?" But moving on doesn't mean acting like everything is as it was. It doesn't mean continuing to force victims to repeatedly interact with those who hurt them. I never want to see my rapist's face again. Too often, narratives around sexual assault and rehabilitation are focused on getting the abuser's life back to normal as quickly as possible, sometimes without them ever having admitted wrongdoing. I dream of a world where questions about justice are centered around the needs of the victim, not about the personal journey, if any, of the rapist.

I don't know if I'm completely okay, or even what "okay" looks like. I'll tell myself I'm fine, only to have moments when I remember how my trust was violated, my selfhood violated, the physical pain I felt, and yes, I still do get angry sometimes. I wonder if I was lying when I told him I forgave him. Are you still allowed to have bad days when you've supposedly moved on? But my priorities have shifted, and my thought process with them. I've learned to replace the torpedo of intrusive questions—*Is what he did really that bad? Has he been appropriately punished? Is he going to do this again?*—with a single, simpler one—*How are you going to take care of yourself today?*—and I remember that I'll be fine. I can always take the elevator back down to the lobby and walk out the door.

About the Editor

Lilly Dancyger is a contributing editor and writing instructor at *Catapult*, assistant books editor at Barrelhouse, and former memoir editor at *Narratively*. She's at work on a memoir about her father's art, heroin addiction, and death, and everything—tangible and not—that she inherited from him. Her essays and features on culture, sex, politics, and literature have appeared in *The Rumpus*, *The Washington Post*, *The Guardian*, *New York* magazine, and more, and she hosts the popular monthly reading series Memoir Monday in Brooklyn. Lilly lives in New York City with her husband and her cat.

About the Contributors

Lisa Marie Basile is a poet, essayist, and editor living in New York City. She's the founding editor in chief of *Luna Luna Magazine* and the author of the poetry collection *Nympholepsy* (Inside the Castle, 2018) and the collection of practices and rituals for intentional living, *Light Magic for Dark Times* (Fair Winds Press, 2018).

Dani Boss is a former high school English teacher who lives in the Pacific Northwest. She has an MFA from Goddard College and is currently at work on a memoir about social class and belonging.

Keah Brown is a journalist and writer whose work can be found in *Glamour*, *Marie Claire UK*, *Harper's Bazaar*, and *Teen Vogue*, among others. Her debut essay collection, *The Pretty One* (Atria Books), was published this year.

Rios de la Luz is a queer Xicana and Chapina living in El Paso. She is the author of the short story collection *The Pulse between Dimensions and the Desert* (Ladybox Books, 2015) and the novella *Itzá* (Broken River Books, 2017). Her work has been featured in *Corporeal Clamor*, *Broadly*, *WEIRD SISTER*, *WOHE LIT*, and *St. Sucia*.

Evette Dionne is the editor in chief of Bitch Media. She's the author of the forthcoming books *Fat Girls Deserve Fairytales Too: Living Hopefully on the Other Side of Skinny* (Seal Press) and *Lifting As We Climb: Black Women's Battle for the Ballot Box* (Viking).

Lisa Factora-Borchers is a Filipina American writer, editor of *Dear Sister: Letters from Survivors of Sexual Violence* (AK Press, 2014), and a contributing editor at *Catapult* magazine. Her work has appeared in several anthologies and online in *The Rumpus*, *The Independent* (UK), *Refinery 29*, *In The Fray*, *Truthout*, *The Feminist Wire*, *International Examiner*, *Mutha* magazine, and *Ano Ba* magazine.

Melissa Febos is the author of the memoir *Whip Smart* (St. Martin's Press, 2010), the essay collection *Abandon Me* (Bloomsbury, 2017), and a second essay collection, *Girlhood*, forthcoming in 2020. Her essays have recently appeared in *Tin House*, *Granta*, *The Believer*, and the *New York Times*.

Anna Fitzpatrick is a freelance writer and the digital media editor of *The Believer*. She lives in Toronto, Canada.

Rowan Hisayo Buchanan is the author of the novels *Harmless Like You* (W. W. Norton, 2017), which won an Authors' Club First Novel Award and a Betty Trask Award, and *Starling Days* (Sceptre, 2019). Her other work appears in *Granta*, *The Atlantic*, and *The Guardian*.

Minda Honey's writing has been featured by *Longreads*, *Oxford American*, *The Washington Post*, *The Guardian*, *Playboy*, *Vice*, and other major publications. She's working on a memoir about dating as a Black woman in Southern California, working title *An Anthology of Assholes*.

Leslie Jamison is the author of the *New York Times* bestsellers *The Recovering* (Little, Brown, 2018) and *The Empathy Exams* (Graywolf Press, 2014), as well as a novel, *The Gin Closet* (Free Press, 2010), and the essay collection *Make It Scream, Make It Burn* (Little, Brown), just released this fall. She is a contributing writer for the *New York Times Magazine* and directs the graduate nonfiction program at Columbia University.

Erin Khar's debut memoir, *Strung Out*, is forthcoming from Park Row Books in 2020. Erin is also the managing editor at *Ravishly*, where she writes the weekly advice column, *Ask Erin*.

Marissa Korbel is the creator and author of *The Thread*, a monthly essay column for *The Rumpus*. Her writing has appeared in numerous publications, including *Harper's Bazaar*, *Guernica*, *Bitch*, and *The Manifest-Station*. She works as a public interest attorney on issues affecting campus and minor sexual assault survivors.

Shaheen Pasha is the co-editor of *Mirror on the Veil: A Collection of Personal Essays on Hijab and Veiling* (Critical, Cultural and Communications Press, 2017), and her work has appeared in the *Dallas Morning News*, *Narratively*, *New England Public Radio*, *USA Today*, *The Daily Beast*, and *Quartz*, among other publications. She is working on a memoir about madness and the Pakistani-American immigrant experience.

Samantha Riedel is a freelance politics and culture writer specializing in transgender issues. Her essays and interviews have previously appeared in *Bitch*, *them.*, *Teen Vogue*, and *Publishers Weekly*. She lives in western Massachusetts, where she is currently at work on her first book.

Sheryl Ring is a consumer rights attorney and the legal director at Open Communities, a not-for-profit legal aid agency serving underprivileged families in the Chicagoland area. Sheryl is a regular contributor to *FanGraphs*, where she focuses on the legal side of baseball; her work has also been featured in *Chicago* magazine and in the forthcoming 2019 *BP Annual* from Baseball Prospectus.

Marisa Siegel lives, writes, and edits near NYC but thinks twenty times a day about heading back west. She holds an MFA in poetry from Mills College in Oakland, California. She is editor in chief and owner of *The Rumpus*.

Megan Stielstra is the author of three collections, most recently *The Wrong Way to Save Your Life* (Harper Perennial, 2017). Her work appears in *Best American Essays*, the *New York Times*, *The Believer*, *Longreads*, *Guernica*, *The Rumpus*, and on National Public Radio. She is currently an artist in residence at Northwestern University.

Nina St. Pierre is a writer and editor with an MFA from Rutgers. Her work has been published in *Catapult*, *Narratively*, *InStyle*, *GOOD*, *Flaunt*, *Bitch*, and *Brooklyn Magazine*. She's finishing a memoir about self-immolation set in rural Northern California and a collection of essays about boundaries via sex and spirituality.

Meredith Talusan's debut memoir, *Fairest*, is forthcoming in spring 2020 from Viking/Penguin Random House.

Monet Patrice Thomas is a poet and writer from North Carolina. She holds an MFA from the Inland Northwest Center for Writers at Eastern Washington University in Spokane, Washington. She is the interviews editor at *The Rumpus*. Her story

"Ring of Salt" was featured in *Best Small Fictions 2018*, chosen by guest editor Aimee Bender.

Reema Zaman is an award-winning author, speaker, actress, and advocate. Born in Bangladesh, raised in Hawaii and Thailand, she presently lives in Oregon. She is the 2018 Oregon Literary Arts' Writer of Color Fellow and author of the memoir *I Am Yours* (Amberjack Press, 2019). Her work has been featured in the *New York Times*, the Dear Sugars podcast, *The Guardian*, *Ms. Magazine*, *The Rumpus*, *Guernica*, *Longreads*, *Narratively*, and elsewhere.